Over a Million Kids Sold -- On What?

The Job Corps Story

Alfred D. Richards

Owings Mills, Maryland

Over a Million Kids Sold -- On What?
The Job Corps Story

Copyright © 1992 Alfred Richards

All rights reserved under International and
Pan-American copyright conventions. No part of this book
may be reproduced, stored in a retrieval system or transmitted
in any form, electronic, mechanical, or other means, now known
or hereafter invented without written permission
of the author. Address all inquiries to the author.

Library of Congress
Cataloging in Publication Data
ISBN 1-56167-094-4

Published by

11419 Cronridge Drive #10
Owings Mills, Maryland 21117

Manufactured in the United States of America

Table of Contents

Dedication	v
Acknowledgements	vii
Introduction	1
Job Corps	2
Job Corps Cost	4
Contractors and Job Corps Centers	6
Screeners (Recruiters)	8
Stories of Negative Life	10
Sex	27
Suicide	31
AIDS	33
Job Corps Students and the Law	35
Higher Education	43
Student's Complaints about Conditions	44
Arrests and Homicides	46
Different Points of View	51
Life After Job Corps	63
Turnabout Is Fair Play	68
Illegal Activity	70
Student Rights	72
Your First Week of Job Corps	73
Checklist for a Better Center	77
Agencies to Contact in Time of Need	81

Dedication

This book is dedicated to the many thousands of young men and women the Job Corps program did not help; and to one of the greatest fathers in the world, Mr. James Richards.

Due to the nature of this book, I deem it necessary not to use real names, in most cases.

Acknowledgements

I alone am responsible for putting this book together, for expressing all opinions that are not directly attributed to somebody else, and for making any errors in the facts collected.

I would like to thank the many good young men and women I had the benefit of knowing for their unseen help in the preparation of this work.

Thanks also to the residential and training staff, the little people who are trying to keep a tired, abused and defective system that is producing defective parts at the taxpayers' expense going. In most cases, they are understaffed, underpaid, and without respect from contractual administrators.

Thank you, too, Johnnye C. Bradley and Alisa M. Hoffman at American Literary Press for your help in producing this book.

Finally, I would like to thank my wife and my children for their patience and understanding.

Introduction

The collection of materials in this book are from my own accounts as told to me by staff members and students. Some of the stories in this book may shock you, but they are just a small piece of the Job Corps puzzle.

I would like to explain why I have written this book. There are many reasons: love of one's fellow human beings, country, family and God -- all the things I found lacking at the Job Corps centers. Oh, the shame I feel inside for being a taxpayer in a country that allows companies to use and abuse government programs, misleading and abusing our children, and profiting from their misfortune of having been born lower class. I would like to say that in all the time I have spent as a residential advisor not a day passed without me asking myself this question: "Does the Job Corps program really work?"

I do not think so! Like a lot of government programs, it is in dire need of repair. During the two years I served Job Corps as a residential advisor on a center numbering 1500 students I can truly say I only saw three students placed in full-time, good paying jobs.

Why do children of the poor continue to pave the road to health, happiness and prosperity for the children of the wealthy? I am not advocating that kids should or should not go to the Job Corps but that they should investigate all other educational programs before taking that step.

Job Corps

Job Corps was established by the Economic Opportunity Act of 1964. The corps was administered by the Office of Economic Opportunity until 1969, when it was transferred to the Department of Labor.

This program is funded by the United States government and is the most costly domestic job training program financed by the federal government. It provides meals, rooms, recreation, medical care, living and readjustment allowances, as well as trade and educational services for disadvantaged teenagers, young men and women. The basic goal of the program is to teach job skills to people who range in age from 16 to 22 years old. The Job Corps also offers counseling, health care and job placement.

In the past, a number of the people who completed the program found a job, returned to school or joined the armed forces. The Job Corps provides these services through its residential centers in the United States and Puerto Rico. Young men and women can stay at a center for six months of training, but some remain as long as two years.

Most of the centers serve people from a particular state or region and design their programs to meet job needs in that locality. At many centers, for example, labor unions offer special apprenticeship programs in such construction trades as brick-laying, carpentry and heavy equipment operation.

I have found in the time I worked for Job Corps and during the writing of this book on the Department of Labor Job Corps programs, all negative factors about the program and its centers are intentionally concealed.

Also, the Department of Labor and its contractors, who are hired to manage the majority of the centers, are constantly bombarded by lawsuits and many of the people in the surrounding communities refer to the Job Corps centers as correctional institutions.

As a residential advisor, I noticed that a large number of the students were leaving the Job Corps center without the training they had come for -- and without a *job*. I also witnessed some shady goings-on between the Department of Labor and its contractors that made me question the mission and control of the Job Corps program. I repeatedly called the Department of Labor offices for information on the Job Corps program and time after time was given the runaround. When I would ask a government employee or representative of the Department of Labor questions in regard to the number of kids entering and completing the Job Corps program, as well as cost figures, they would become very defensive and unresponsive, saying they did not know or they did not have this information handy -- all vague and elusive answers. The questions I asked were all public information they should have known.

Job Corps Cost

Actual and estimated budgets for the past six years:

1987 $640,173,000 (actual budget)
1988 $656,859,000 (actual budget)
1989 $741,731,000 (actual budget)
1990 $774,470,000 (actual budget)
1991 $821,989,000 (estimated budget)
1992 $866,731,000 (estimated budget)

Where does the money go?

Center operations contractors like M.T.C.	74.7%
Students allowances	9.0%
Outreach, screening, placement	4.4%
Construction/acquisition of new centers	3.5%
Student transportation	5.0%
Other costs	7.2%

Center Operation Costs

Administration/Management	39.6%
Residential living area	33.1%
Vocational Training (welding, painting, auto trades, etc.)	14.6%
Basic Education (reading, math, GED)	7.2%
Medical Care	5.5%

Estimated cost per student

	Yearly	Daily
1987	$15,800	$43.00
1988	$16,200	$44.00
1989	$18,100	$50.00
1990	$18,900	$52.00
1991	$20,100	$55.00
1992	$21,100	$57.00

Information provided by the U.S. government Office of Management and Budget. Fiscal years 1987-1992.

Job Corps' estimated lifetime student full program completion rate for the past 25 years has been less than 20% of the total student enrollment.

One out of five kids who enter the gates of Job Corps center ever complete the full program -- high school/GED certificate and trade. As of the 90s, the estimated number of kids departing the Job Corps program without completing it has been as high as 80%.

It is estimated that it costs the government and taxpayers upwards of $100 thousand per year for one of Job Corps's full program completion students to graduate.

Less than one percent of the kids who enter the Job Corps program are placed in a full-time, well-paying job by the placement service.

Contractors and Job Corps Centers

Job Corps is administered by the U.S. Department of Labor. Individual centers may be managed by either government agencies such as the Department of Agriculture, Department of Interior and the Bureau of Reclamation or by private companies like Management and Training Corporation which operated Clearfield Job Corps Center, the second largest.

During the peak enrollment season from September to March, this center will maintain over 1500 students, usually well over its max, which often changes with a stroke of a pen.

The center in Clearfield, Utah, provides just about everything. It is supposed to be designed like a small city. The Corps members (students) which they are so frequently called, learn a trade in areas like welding, food service, automotive repair, auto body, carpentry, wood working, etc. The types of kids who attend Job Corps are high school grads and dropouts, as well as problem kids from broken homes and run-ins with the law, and drug problem cases which often involve all types of drugs and alcohol addiction. The responsibility of a contractor doesn't change much from one contractor to another. But the way they handle their responsibility often does.

Management and Training Corporation (MTC) as a contractor for the Department of Labor supervises the running of the Department of Labor programs in connection with management of the facility, personnel, and students' learning programs.

Contractors are supposed to be held accountable for the number of students not completing the program, but this has not been the case. In fact, MTC has been given more contracts by the Department of Labor to manage other Job Corps centers throughout the United States. The idea of the Job Corps program is to help these kids to get into the workforce with a trade and a chance at a productive life.

But as you will learn from reading my book, this is not always the case. In fact, out of the thousands of kids who have passed through the Job Corps center gates, less than 50% leave with a trade, high school diploma or GED. And out of that number, less than 5% are placed in a full-time, permanent job and their employers have found their training to be poor at best.

I hope this book will help the reader better understand what has gone on and what still goes on inside most Job Corps centers.

A number of these contractors are made up of investors who years ago would have been putting their cash in the stock market for security. But as of lately the market has proven to be unreliable. So, because of the shortcomings of the economy, some have created companies and are encouraging investors to invest in a more sure, stable market -- the government.

MTC and companies like it are doing whatever it takes to turn a buck. As one of the main contractors for the Department of Labor, they can receive up to $15,000 for every student who stays in their program 90 days or longer. With the problem of rising unemployment because of the closing of businesses, banks and family-owned farms, contractors see nothing but smooth sailing ahead.

Job Corps attempts to cover up the drug and crime problems that plague many of its centers. Residents who live in the counties who come in contract with Job Corps center students are often aware of the crime fallout of living next to a large Job Corps complex of 1000 plus students. Some of the centers under the control of MTC are Woodstock, Clearfield, Turner, Red Rock, Tongue Point, Charleston, Denison and Keystone. As of 1992, MTC was the number one operator of Job Corps centers, employing around 4,000 part- and full-time employees. Controlling 46 of the total 102 centers, MTC has found security and profit in the Department of Labor Job Corps Programs, a program brought about in the beginning to provide education and jobs for the youth of the country.

Job Corps screeners are often prone to not always telling the truth. They target poor whites and low income minority people. Most often, they work hand-in-hand with the Job Corps contractor in their area or for one to whom the recruiter has close ties. But under the control of some contractors the screener will do or say whatever it takes to fill the Job Corps centers to their maximum because to them and the contractor with whom they associate, they must show a need if the Job Corps program is to grow. They often refer to this kind of recruiting as job security and they are successful at what they do. Every kid is fair game: the mentally ill, drug abusers, rapists, prostitutes, etc.

Handicapped kids are taken in for the sole purpose of improving the image of the center, while the recruiters know these handicapped students have a one in 100 chance of completing the programs and one third that number of being placed in a full time job. Most often the larger, more uncontrollable centers prove to be their dismay, but they continue to send them there.

In the 90s, economic times are harder than ever before and our teenagers, young men and women, are caught right in the middle. We as parents can no longer say to them, "Why don't you get a job?" because nowadays that phrase is becoming a difficult one to quote when we as parents do not have one.

Some of the criteria for joining Job Corps:

Age

You must be at least 16 years of age and not yet 22 years of age. Proof of age such as a birth certificate, driver's license, state I.D., current passport, blessing or baptism certificate is necessary.

Income

You must be low income or come from a low income family. You are eligible if you or your family receives food stamps, welfare, medical card, tribal dividends, unemployment compensation or if you are a ward of the court or state. Applicants who are not on public assistance must provide proof of income over the past 12 months, check stubs, a W-2 form and a letter from an employer.

Court Status If you have a criminal court record your application must be approved by the regional office of the Department of Labor.

Residency You must be a legal resident of the U.S. and must provide proof such as a birth certificate or alien card (green card).

Probation You can remain on probation while in the program as long as the probation office agrees.

Medical If you had psychological counseling during the past two years, medical problems during the past four years, or take psychological medication your application must be approved by the D.O.I.

Stories of Negative Life

The heart of Job Corps is the residential living. Without it, Job Corps would not exist. Residential advisors outnumber all other staff positions on centers. They hear and handle just about everything that happens on center. They act as father, mother and big brother and sister for as many as 40 to 80 young men and women per dormitory.

1. At 2 a.m. bed check, corps member Mike was found to be absent from center (AFC). At 6:45 corps member William was packed out, after failing to return to center for the past two days per instruction from supervisor Unit 16 Bill Dakota. During the pack out conducted by residential advisor (RA) Mr. Anderson and Shanti Potters, they found a large amount of marijuana along with three packs of rolling papers, a homemade drug pipe, and an iron belonging to Job Corps. Also discovered were office supplies belonging to Job Corps -- eight flashlight batteries, one flashlight, post-it note pads, a pool cue and chalk. He also had a large bag of approximately 50 bars of hand soap belonging to a local motel. The drug related items along with the bag of marijuana are attached to this report in a plastic bag. Two "credit" lists were also discovered.

2. Corps member refused to perform dorm J (job). Corps member has been counseled on several occasions concerning his duty in the dorm. Other days he neglected his duty are: 4/24, 4/27 and 4/29. This is becoming a constant problem, his odor making the students in his cube very upset.

3. David reported to the RA at 11:00 a.m. that his walkman had been stolen. He fell asleep last night around 11:00 p.m. and found someone had unplugged his earphones and taken his walkman and battery charger while he laid there in bed. Walkman is black and engraved under the belt clip. Serial numbers are in his file. David paid $30.00 for this walkman.

10

4. Corps member Guevara failed to perform his dorm J in a satisfactory manner on the following dates this past week: 7/25, 7/26, 7/27 and 7/28. On each of these dates the dorm lost points on the daily dorm inspection. Direct result of corps member Guevara's performance was the creation of a very poor sanitary living environment here in D Dorm. Corps member has been counseled on several occasions. Last night about 2:35 a.m. corps member entered my office complaining someone put shaving cream in his bed.

5. Corps member is constantly oversleeping and will not get out of bed until after 7:00 a.m. every morning. He has also refused to perform J. Corps member is gay and was found more than once in other students' beds. He has been counseled on several occasions concerning his duty and sexual activities on center.

6. Corps member Morales and another unidentified corps member were observed by RA turning off circuit breakers to entire dorm. This is the second night in a row this has happened. At approximately 2:30 a.m. corps member Morales and corps members Helen and Arriola poured water in hallway creating a safety hazard and were unnecessarily rude to RA causing Arriola to be placed in another dorm for duration of the night. Corps member Morales refused to go to bed at the given time. He was running up and down the hall and in and out of the cubes. He also made a threat toward his RA according to other corps members in the dorm.

7. Found Baker shooting dice with Brown. This is not the first time. I have asked him several times to go to bed and stop smoking in the restricted areas. He just continues to ignore me and does as he pleases, running around behind Brown and Chad like a little lost puppy. Even after security had taken him to Room 2 (on-center lock up) and took the dice directly from Baker, he continued to deny he had them.

8. Corps member Raymond used a book of matches to set a can of Right Guard on fire. He singed a bed spread on another corps member's bed as he slept, setting off the fire alarm. For this offense he was terminated from the center.

9. Albert's Attempted Suicide. Student Garcia's statement: As I was walking down the hall on my way to my cube, there was someone looking for Albert so I decided to go to his cube to see if he was there and to let him know someone was looking for him. As I entered his room I noticed him sitting on his bed in the room all alone, looking very depressed. I tried talking to him but he was in no mood for talking. I left the room to tell the guy that was looking for him Albert was in his cube. After I told the guy Albert was upset and in no mood for talking the guy left.

Then I returned to Albert's cube just in time to see him going for the glass cleaner. Ron his roommate attempted to stop him but before he could, Albert had ripped the top off the bottle of window cleaner and taken two large swallows. As Ron grabbed the bottle and proceeded to pull it away from Albert I could see it was too late. Albert's legs were starting to buckle. He began shaking all over. His eyes went from a clear white to a cherry red. Then Albert turned as if to be saying goodbye as his eyes rolled back in his head. Then he dropped to the floor. Ron grabbed him before he could hit the floor, then yelled for me to go get the RA, Mr. Robertson. When I entered the RA's office Mr. Robertson and Mr. Black were there. I told them what had just taken place, then I ran back to see if I could help. When Mr. Robertson and Mr. Black arrived two or three minutes had passed.

Student Ron's statement: I was on my way back from the phone room and as I entered the cube, before I could sit down, Albert asked if I could go to the water fountain and get him a cup of water. When I returned I handed him the water and then laid down on my bunk farthest from him. Albert said, "I am going to take this whole thing." He held up a small white envelope in his left hand and then he poured the contents of the envelope into his right hand. I could see the envelope was issued by the Job Corps drugstore.

I shouted, "What the hell are you doing, man?!" Then Albert ran toward the dresser and picked up a bottle of window cleaner, broke off the top to the bottle and put the pills he had in one hand in his mouth. At that time I jumped off the bed and started for him, but before I could stop him, he had taken two large gulps. I grabbed the bottle, then Albert and I wrestled for control of it. The contents of the bottle were splashing all over the place. All the time he was trying to take another gulp. I pushed him back against the lockers and then he let go of the bottle. I think the effects of the pills and the window cleaner were starting to work on him. He just stood there looking at me then his legs gave way and he fell over, but before he could hit the floor I caught him and laid him down.

RA statement: Albert was taken to the nearest hospital's intensive care unit where he was listed in guarded condition. The doctor's report stated Albert would have a full recovery but he had suffered some severe liver damage. Albert was one of our best students; he was the dorm's Vice President. But receiving news that his girlfriend back home was dumping him for another guy was more than he could take mentally. After his release from the hospital he was terminated from Job Corps.

10. Melius was teasing Edward and threw a book at him. Then Edward went to his locker, got a knife and pulled it on Melius. At that time, one of the students who was watching ran to the RA's office to report to Mr. Johnson what was going on. When RA Johnson went to the cube to get the knife from Edward, he found paraphernalia. When the supervisor Mrs. Johnson asked student Edward if they could search his locker, he agreed. More weapons and paraphernalia were found such as a star, rope with a hangman's noose, sharpened screw drivers and a homemade dope pipe.

11. Corps member (CM) Howard entered his cube today at 3:30 p.m. to discover his lock gone and his radio missing from his locker.

12. CM Mays was reported as writing graffiti inside the dormitory. Mays was called to the RA's office and confronted. He would not admit doing the graffiti in question, but we found a paper on top of May's locker identical to the graffiti written in the dorm.

13. Statement by student K.O.: I had just come in the dorm after being on a 32 hour pass and as I proceeded to pass the day room, students Scott, Roscoe and Smith pulled me into the day room and started hitting me. As they did so, they kept asking me what I did with Bill's lighter. They stopped hitting me just long enough for me to say I didn't have it. They started hitting me again and again. Luckily, student Shawn came in just before Roscoe was about to hit me in the face with a leg he had just ripped from the coffee table. Shawn said, "Stop! What's going on?" They told him they were just playing around. He said, "This doesn't look like playing to me," then he made them stop. I then went to my cube to lay down and try to put what had just happened behind me.

I laid there smoking a cigarette just about to fall asleep when it happened. Scott, Roscoe, Jackson, Smith and Edward entered my cube. I didn't see them enter, but as the blanket came over my head I pulled it back just enough to get a look at them. A stick came crashing down on my head. They assaulted me with their fists and that stick for about 30 seconds before my roommate started waking up from the sound of my crying out for help. But he said they were out of the room before he could see who it was.

14. Cradle Robbing. Sexual interaction between staff and students is not permitted but continues frequently. Ms. Romeo, RA of E Dorm, while working midnight shift, decided to drop in on the RA of H Dorm to pick up a file folder on a student who was moved from H Dorm to E Dorm. As Ms. Romeo entered H Dorm and headed for the RA's office, she noticed that the door to the office was closed and that there were strange noises coming from within.

She knocked on the door but no one answered, so she proceeded to open the door. As the door opened Ms. Romeo noticed the lights were out. As she looked around the room, to her surprise there were two people on the floor with all their clothing off having sex. They were so involved with one another that they didn't notice Ms. Romeo until she said "What the f--- is going on here!" The two people jumped up from the floor with only their goose bumps to cover them. Ms. Romeo could see clearly that one of them was the female RA of H Dorm who usually works the day shift, who had been forced to work a double because the night RA called in sick.

Mrs. Kennedy is an overweight 45 year old married woman with three children from ages 10 to 20. The other person on the floor was her 17 year old student lover. There had been rumors going around center that Mrs. Kennedy had a student lover, but now she was caught in the act. Center rules forbid dating or interaction between staff and students. Mrs. Kennedy pleaded with Ms. Romeo not to turn her in, but Ms. Romeo just turned and walked away. She always disliked her and now this was her chance to get even. Ms. Romeo reported the incident to her supervisor and two days later Mrs. Kennedy was terminated from employment. Her husband moved out with the kids and filed for a divorce.

Three weeks later Ms. Romeo, a 34 year old divorced mother of two, was found to be having an on-going off center affair with a 20 year old student. It was later found out she was a drug and alcohol dealer on center. She let one of the students, a female who had been terminated from Job Corps for trying to commit suicide by hanging herself from the shower, live rent free with her because she was the sister of Ms. Romeo's student lover, Melvin.

Once, Melvin had gone home to Kansas on a center paid home leave for three weeks. Ms. Romeo saw that as her opportunity to break off her relationship with him. On his return, Melvin was very upset when he heard she had another lover, so student Melvin tried to use the affair he had with Ms. Romeo to win her back, but she refused to give in. He notified center security to search her car for drugs and alcohol. They found nothing. He would follow her around everywhere, calling her both at work and home. Things got so bad that she had to take two weeks of vacation time to let everything blow over.

But during that two week period she let her new student lover borrow her car. He said that he was just going to the store, but what he neglected to tell her was that the store was in the next state almost 75 miles away. On his return, the car went off the road, flipped over twice and was totaled. The police investigation got back to center security and the center management forced Ms. Romeo to resign.

15. Defecated in Fireplace. Dung, age 19, entered the dorm around 12:30 p.m. Center curfew time on the weekend is 12:00 p.m. He was intoxicated and was advised by the RA to report to bed and stay there until morning. Dung is Vietnamese and has only been in this country for eight months, a student of Job Corps about half that time, and doesn't understand English very well. But he did go to bed. Ten minutes later he was throwing up on the student sleeping in the bunk beneath him, then he went to sleep in his vomit. Thirty minutes later he fell out of his bed and went into the day room where he fell asleep on the floor in front of the fire place. One of the students reported seeing him there. This morning we found a pile of human feces in the fire place. No one saw who did it but it is alleged that Dung was the only one who could have.

Some of the students are upset over this and are trying to take matters into their own hands. When confronted by the RA Dung refused to reply. Minutes after leaving the RA's office and returning to his cube he was harassed by the students of the dorm to the point where he became so enraged that he ran out of the dorm and off the center grounds, with only one sock on his foot and no shoes, when it was 25 degrees outside, leaving everything else behind, never to return. His clothes and things were given away to charity.

16. Space Tripping. At 12:15 a.m. found corps member Foster in the day room all alone sitting in a corner of the room with all the lights out, not uttering a sound. I turned on the lights and asked

him if everything was alright -- "You know it's well past downtime. Do you have a problem you would like to talk about?" Foster didn't reply; he just sat there with a spaced-out look on his face. I tried repeatedly to get him to go to his room but with no luck; Foster just stayed there. I returned to the RA's office to ask Ms. Victor to talk to him. She was about to get off work for the night but still had a few minutes. She tried to get him to go to his room but with very little luck also. We called the supervisor. He in turn called security and they tried to communicate with him. The supervisor said, "Foster should be placed in the infirmary because he is high off something." As security was putting Foster in handcuffs, one of Foster's roommate's came forward to inform us that student Foster had been sniffing paint thinner and glue and he could be having a reaction. Foster was taken to the infirmary and remained there handcuffed most of the night. The next day he was terminated from the center, dropped off at the nearest bus station like damaged and returned merchandise.

This is a letter written to the manager of health services by an RA who was fired soon after writing it. "I wish to take the time to express to you my displeasure and concern regarding how corps member Foster's situation was handled. On the night of May 12, student Foster appeared to be on some sort of psycho-toxic chemical. He was uncooperative and had to be removed forcibly from his living area. This student was obviously, even to a layman, very mentally unstable and continued to attempt to inflict injury upon himself. When questioned, the student continued to speak of an inner voice telling him to hurt himself. Several staff members involved in this incident were obviously under the misconception student Foster would be cared for properly if taken to the infirmary.

"Our mental health consultants should have been utilized for proper handling of these kinds of situations to be in the best interest of our students' well being. Instead, I was amazed to learn the nurse on duty gave Foster a choice of remaining in the infirmary if he was good or being locked in security until morning. I don't question the nurse's capabilities as a nurse because I know she's very good at meeting a student's physical needs, however, a student's mental or emotional state is a different area and should require a decision made by someone more qualified in that particular field. Keep in mind that a wrong decision could have drastic effects resulting in injuries to both students and staff which could result in lawsuits that could have been avoided.

"If the RN is making these decisions then why have an on-call mental health staff? My concern is that an unstable student was just sent to bed with only one infirmary staff on duty which could have resulted in the student hurting himself or others. I feel we have not only compromised the safety and well being of the staff, but the safety and well being of all the students. If things continue, maybe we need to look at some new policies regarding the use of our mental health services team. Please be aware that they weren't notified at all. How can we be sure that the decision we made was the one they would have made? Why do we have them if we don't use them?..."

The next day, the student was terminated. The following week the RA was dismissed.

17. Monica's Late Night. Monica was on her way back to the Job Corps center after a day-long sight seeing and buying trip in town with her friends Mark and Sally. They were having a great time. "I think that weird looking guy is following us," said Monica.

Mark replied, "Don't worry about him. He's just one of those fuckin' fags. If he comes this way I'll kick his fag ass! Besides, he's going the other way; he's not following us. You're just imagining it."

Sally said, "Let's get out of the mall. It's getting late. We don't want to miss the last bus back to the center."

"You guys go ahead. I saw a nice, cute outfit back there at that last store we were in and I'm going to get it before some other bitch beats me to it. I'll meet you back there." Monica got her outfit but missed the bus and had to take the local city bus that did not pass by Job Corps center. In fact, none of the city buses passed within two miles of the center. The city bus was the last one for the night. It was full to the max -- so full that from where Monica was sitting she couldn't see some of the people on board and the driver had to make a lot of stops. When Monica's stop came, she exited with three or four other people. One of them was the strange kid she thought was following her back at the mall. He walked down the road she was on to Job Corps. It was very late and the road was dark because it had no street lights. Monica became afraid, so she went to a small convenience store just across the street from the bus stop. She asked the store clerk if she could use the telephone.

"You people always come in here trying to get something for nothing. If you're not stealing my stuff you're begging for it. Get out of here. There's a pay phone outside!" the clerk replied.

"But mister, there's a guy following me!"

"I don't care if it's Jack the Ripper! Get out of here, bitch, before I call the police on you, understand!"

Monica went to the pay phone and called Job Corps. It was very late now -- around 1:00 am. The phone rang six times before someone answered. "Hello, security, Jim. Can I help you?"

"Sir, my name is Monica and I am a student there but I missed the last bus returning to center and had to take the city bus. Now there's a guy following me and I'm afraid that he's going to fuck with me. Do you think someone could come down here to the convenience store and pick me up please?"

"You missed the bus and now you expect us to come and get you? I do not have the staff to go off center to pick up every student who calls in here needing a ride back to center. You better stop playing around young lady and start walking"

"But sir, I am not playing around. I need help!" Monica said.

Click! The guy at security had hung up on her. Monica called back once more with no luck. The store was closing and as the store owner left he gave Monica a dirty look and said, "Look here, bitch, you better get away from my store. Now!"

She looked down the road and didn't see the guy anywhere. Like a ghost in the night he sprang from the dark, hitting her in the head. She tried to escape but he grabbed her and threw her to the ground. He pulled her down the side of a hill with one hand and hit her with the other. Monica shouted for help until her throat was dry. She glanced around when he wasn't hitting her in the face and she could see the car lights as they passed on the road above them. As they did so, she cried out to them, but he put his hand over her mouth so tight she could not breathe.

Monica doesn't remember what happened next because she blacked out. When she awoke, she was in the hospital. Monica quit the program with no trade or high school diploma and returned home to Cincinnati, Ohio. Her attacker was never found.

18. Tale of the Missing Boy. The is the story of the student who was said to have walked off center in the fall of 1974 and was never heard of again. This story has been told by students and staff and passed along as all stories go. Our story began with an Indian boy by the name of John, age 18. He was involved in a fight with another boy in an area that is now known as Blood Alley. During the fight John looked as though he was winning. As he held the other guy down, someone hit him in the head with a rock. It is said that someone was the other kid's girlfriend and that John died and was buried someplace around the gymnasium with that rock still embedded in his head.

The center management has repeatedly said the story is untrue, and that it is not Job Corps' responsibility once a student leaves or quits and walks out the front gate. Some students say they have seen him -- a ghostly figure wearing green coveralls (trade suit) walking around one of two places, either the gym or the backside of the cafeteria (Blood Alley).

19. A Beginning. Damion (Detour) enjoyed a life in Compton, one of Los Angeles' most demanding communities. He lived in a two bedroom apartment with his mother, younger sister and his older brother by three years who had moved out to live with his older girlfriend but drops in from time to time when he gets low on money or needs a place to chill out. Damion was walking home from school in the company of his best friend Fred Jackson (Tee Pe). The neighborhood was decorated with the loving care that only gangs can do. Graffiti and bullet holes riddled walls;

broken glass, trash littered the street covering the cracked pavement for months before the city street department gets around to it. But no sooner do they clean it up than the next day the street looks the same. People come and go; drug dealers stand on just about every corner. You can get it all here -- cocaine, crank, crack, blow, dope, heroin, horse -- you name it, the narcotics are here -- different guys every day selling the same things.

Fred (Tee Pe) was carrying his big box his uncle had given him two weeks ago after hitting the three box lotto. Tee Pe was carrying it like a proud father of a newborn baby boy, with the volume turned about three quarters of the way up, playing the only tape he had titled "Poison". A dark red late 70s model Ford with heavily tinted windows moving at a very slow rate of speed turned the corner and positioned itself directly behind the two boys. The music from Tee Pe's boom box was so loud they didn't hear the engine of the car which could have warned them of the approaching danger.

The rear window of the car rolled down as if it was powered electrically, and a double barrel shotgun appeared. Others on the street had noticed the car and what was about to happen and started ducking and running for cover. Damion and Tee Pe turned around to see what was going on and as they did so the gunman in the smoked glass car opened fire, centering it full force on Tee Pe. The blast picked him up and knocked him back about ten feet into and through the meat market's front window, sending glass flying everywhere. The gun barrel was still hanging out the window of the car smoking like a mad bull on a cold winter morning. The car drove away slowly as if the occupants were admiring their handiwork before departing. Even as they did so, Damion crawled over to Tee Pe. "Are you all right?"

The ground was covered with blood! Tee Pe's blood! His body had large pieces of glass sticking everywhere. He was not breathing and when Damion touched him his body was cool. His closest friend was dead! The fatal shots were fired by Damion's brother's rival gang. They left Tee Pe dead and Damion in serious condition with shotgun pellets in the legs and right shoulder, glass cuts on hands, arms and face. Also, a little girl who was shopping inside the meat market got hit by a stray pellet which struck her in the back, crippling her for life. The next day Damion's brother's gang countered, killing three members of the other gang. His brother was arrested and charged with the murder of two of them and now faces 20 years to life.

Incidents of violence between gangs happens on a daily basis here. On the surface things may look all right one day, but underneath the question isn't when but where will trouble strike next and who will die. By the time help arrives it's always too late. The word in the hood is that the police have orders to wait until the gang members are through fighting before arriving. As Damion and his mother rode home from the hospital he could tell something was on her mind. "Mom, is everything cool?"

"Son, I am afraid for you. Now that your brother is gone they will be coming for you to continue where he left off. I have tried hard to keep you away from the gangs. Damion, I don't make enough money for us all to move but you can. I talked to that man at the Job Corps recruiting center and he said you could go today if you wanted to."

"But Mom, what will happen to you and Tasha? Who will help and look out for you two once I have gone?"

"Son, I have been taking care of this family ever since your dad and I broke up nine years ago and I will continue until I can't take another breath. You do as I ask. Leave before it's too late!"

As the taxi turned the corner to the street their apartment was on, they saw mayhem and pandemonium everywhere. He thought, *There has to be something better than this.* "Stop. I'll go."

His mother turned to the driver and said, "Please take us downtown." Damion was soon on a plane headed to one of the west's largest training centers.

20. Female student received a large amount of money from an inheritance, bought a van, loaded it up with her friends and had a party that lasted a week. Drugs and alcohol influenced their every move. On the last day of that week along a highway before

turning back to Job Corps, they were exiting a freeway off-ramp going in excess of 70 mph. She lost control of the van and it turned over several times before smashing into a bridge embankment. All the students in the van were pronounced DOA (dead on arrival). It took a total of three hours to remove them from the wreckage.

21. The old adage has it that misery simply enjoys company...so, deep in pain, I called the name of some funky-fied friends of mine. We were kickin' back in the old Red Shack, smoking and grooving to a contemporary beat and the sound was much alive. The atmosphere of the shack is quite serene. My thoughts are of a profound state of euphoria. Perhaps this is due to the psychologically altering THC factor. In many unexplained ways, one could view the Red Shack as some sort of sanctuary dimension. There I sit, silently content on a boxed crate and groove. My sole desire is to improve my inner galactic state of affairs, although the sequence of passage may appear as though my primary function is to consistently rap 'n' rhyme. But at the same time in actuality, my good friend corruption comes to substantiate the fact that the life of Lil' Magic had been foreclosed upon prematurely, unethically and without motive. When corruption informed me of this I was in a dream-like trance.

It wasn't until the following morning that the impact took its toll. Vividly I recalled the refried confusion of yesterday. In short, it was total chaos. The retention of it all exploded in my face as I read the morning headlines: "Gang Member Slain in Compton." By no means was Magic affiliated with the subcultural ways of the Red Shack.

He devised a personal constitution for himself and played life by the rules. Unlike the rest of us so-called role models, he didn't believe in inebriation, weapons or drugs. I surmise that his obsession for red began when he was granted a basketball scholarship to U.N.L.V. We all envied him. Subconsciously, we wanted what he had. Undoubtedly, if anyone was able to escape the vice of the ghetto, he was a prime candidate. Even the children recognized him as being a product of great potential.

However, as a result of him representing a color, the tabloids portrayed him as being a culprit who inevitably became the victim of his own circumstances. Far worse, just another black statistic who had succumbed from a fatal gunshot wound, nothing more than a number to be subtracted from society.

The student who wrote this was terminated for selling drugs, fighting and violating curfew (all associated with his abuse of alcohol), just weeks from completing high school. He was a 20 year old black kid from the streets of L.A. with nothing to look forward to but Job Corps. Before coming to JC he was living his life as a homeless person on the streets of Los Angeles after a stay of eight months in the L.A. County Jail for stealing boxes of canned food from a loading dock. But now he's back on the street living the life of a dog because his only problem was that he loved the freedom and peace that comes with being an alcoholic.

22. Home Boy Cooking. Time: 12:15 a.m. Most of the students are up and about because it's the weekend and they usually do not have to be in bed until 2 a.m. Student David entered my office to ask me if he could use the pay telephone. The pay phone is not supposed to be in use after 12 a.m. without RA approval. David went on to inform me that he was upset because his brother to whom he gave his business before coming to Job Corps was about to do something stupid. He was going to go against David's advice and make a drug deal with a guy David had a bad deal with which ended in David having to kill one of the guy's soldiers and David's friend, Boxer, getting shot in the leg. But this guy got away without a scratch.

I gave David the go ahead to use the phone as long as he kept his conversation short and kept me informed of the situation.

Time: 12:30 a.m. David informs me he had called some friends of his to back up his dumb brother and to make sure nothing went wrong with the deal.

Time: 12:50 a.m. David was repeating to himself in a loud tone of voice, "I know something is going to go wrong. If that motherfucker tries to fuck over my brother I'll kill him. David continued raving up and down the hallway going in and out cubes, talking to his friends.

Time: 1:15 a.m. David's back on the phone trying to reach his brother with no luck. He becomes very upset, runs down the hallway yelling, "I knew it! That motherfucker! Motherfucker!" and into cube 6. You could hear David yelling and carrying on in a childish manner through the dormitory. This type of behavior isn't uncommon in a dorm of this size -- 73 students, four to eight to a cube.

In this type of situation, the RA calls the student into his office to talk over any problems the student is having. So I called David to the office for the second time that night and asked him how things were coming along with that problem back home. He was still upset and very emotional almost to the point of tears. In a way it kind of took me by surprise because David was a big strong kid for age 18 and to look at him you would think he was a lot older. He was a "take charge" kind of kid who wasn't afraid to fight if he had to and he made that point very clear throughout the center. Yes, he was and is a gang member, but I am sure that was one decision he had little or no choice in making. When he talked, his voice cracked and as I looked into his eyes I could tell he was on some kind of drug. That was more of a surprise because David was a dealer of drugs on center but seldom used them.

I asked, "David, what's going on? Come on, you can tell me."

"Mr. Miller, I knew the shit wasn't right! Because if it was, somebody would have called me by now. Mr. Miller I got to get out of this fuckin' place! I know I should have killed that motherfucker when I had the chance."

"David, don't worry about something unnecessarily before you have all the facts. Why don't you call someone back home to see how things went?" Fifteen minutes later he returned. "Mr. Miller, I knew it. I called my boy D.C. He and Waco drove by the place where the deal went down and they said there were cops all over the place. They were able to scope out the situation and found out there was a big shoot out and two people were dead and three others have been taken to the hospital in bad condition. Please, God, don't let one of the dead motherfuckers be my brother."

"David, why don't you get some rest? I'll wake you if someone calls."

"Fuck that! I don't think I could sleep now. I got to get home and take care of some unfinished business. This time I won't miss that motherfucker."

David went to his cube and remained there until 2:15 a.m. before returning to the phone room and calling to check on the condition of his brother. After talking for about ten minutes he walked into the RA office to talk to me. "Mr. Miller, my brother is not one of the dead, but he is in the hospital in critical condition in a coma with a bullet in his back. And that motherfucker got away again. But I got some of my guys out looking for him hauling some heavy artillery. I'm tired Mr. Miller. I think I'll crash out in the day room."

The next day David was involved in a fight where the other kid was put in the hospital suffering from three broken ribs and a slight concussion. David was sent home pending a center review board disciplinary hearing. He never returned.

23. Down Stream. Student Running Water was found a few miles away from the center face down in a river bed. Police investigation concluded his death was accidental. He was last seen going over the fence heading for the river that runs along the side of the center. Coroner's report stated his blood alcohol level was five times the legal limit. Student was terminated for failure to return to center due to dying.

Sex

I have found that when it comes to making love students will do it in just about every place imaginable -- under bushes, in trash dumpsters, on roof tops, in swimming pools, on top of picnic tables, in the ceilings, even in the open in front of everyone and more and more we are finding male students in female dormitories under and in their beds. Sex is a problem that is uncontrollable because on most centers the men outnumber the women five or even ten to one and the selling of sex is very common on and off center. In fact, the student prostitute has a better life living on center than on the street.

Cheap sex? Wanna have some, go to Job Corps. It may not be clean but it sure is plentiful because there aren't anything but whores out there. "One of the bitches gave me the crabs," is the cry of one returning male student after a trip home and a visit with his own doctor.

Sexual Harassment

There is little regard given to the female students in the areas of respect and mannerism by a majority of the male students and staff population. The female students are frequently referred to as bitches, whores, hoes, teasers, sluts and prostitutes. Male students treat females as sexual objects and frequently refer to them as such.

Usually, once they have had sex with a female they will boast and brag about it to their friends and just about anyone who cares to listen. They have a "love 'em and leave 'em" attitude. Once a new female or male arrives on center he or she is checked out by some of the male and female students. If a girl or boy has the misfortune of good looks and no street smarts, they will try their damnedest to take advantage of the newcomers, in most cases by trying to become their friend in hopes of leading them into a lifestyle of drugs, prostitution or homosexual behavior.

Prostitution

Prostitution is nothing new. It has been around forever, but the things that go on in and around some of the Job Corps centers are beyond belief. Females and males both are targeted by flesh peddling opportunists who seem to lurk in and around the centers. They are usually accompanied by their counterparts, the drug pushers. I have found the small living allowance the students receive every two to three weeks which runs between $10.00 to $50.00 before center deduction doesn't go very far, but if subsidized by prostitution, a kid could live very well on and off center.

Usually, once a student quits, is terminated or completes out from the Job Corps program, a number of them remain in the surrounding communities.

Rape, Molestation and Sexual Child Abuse

There is an alarming number of students under the age of 18 on Job Corps centers who have become the target of older male and female students as well as adults on and off center with the use of drugs, alcohol, sex or money. They will try to entice newcomers into participating in sexual acts both of the heterosexual and homosexual nature.

A Case of Student Sexual Abuse

Student Tunson, a new student, was found by A Irene Right. As she entered his cube, she was shocked to witness three of the dorm's white students hounding student Tunson (also white) down on the floor with his underwear down. They were raping him with a mop handle. Student Tunson was removed from that dorm and put in another dorm under Protective Custody (PC) where he remained until his termination. An on-center investigation revealed this was the third tim student Tunson had been raped in that manner in the past four weeks since coming to Job Corps from a rural community that was suffering economic hard times. Because of his academic shortcomings, the other students referred to him as the backward kid, hillbilly or hick.

The Case of the Reformed Prostitute

Tracy was 16 when she made the decision to go to Job Corps after living a life of prostitution and drug abuse on the streets of Kansas City, Missouri and after being put out of her apartment after her mother was picked up for selling drugs and put in jail for one to five years. Children's services put her in a foster home but she was sexually abused by an older boy who lived there. After leaving the foster home she found one of her mother's old girlfriends by the name of TC who let her stay with her only if she could pay her way. TC introduced Tracy to Donnie the pimp who in turn introduced Tracy to drugs and prostitution. Two months later, Tracy was arrested for prostitution and turned over to the juvenile court where she was given a choice of remaining in juvenile hall until her 18th birthday or joining Job Corps and remaining on probation for one year. After thinking about leaving a lifestyle that was taking her nowhere, Tracy enrolled.

Tracy was a model student. She made a 180 degree turn around once given the opportunity to change. In two years' time she completed high school and two trades: retail sales and health occupations. After leaving Job Corps and returning home, she moved in with her mother. Now she was 18 and was determined to make something of her life. She was able to find a job as a nurse's aid in a local nursing home for the elderly and made plans to attend college in the fall. Six weeks later she received the readjustment check of about $1000.00 and moved into her own apartment. She met a nice Christian guy at a local church and within a year they were making plans to get married and start a family.

Everything was going great for Tracy until the day she received a letter from the health department marked confidential. Tracy opened the letter and read, "We are sorry to inform you that a recent sexual partner of yours at Job Corps has tested positive with the infectious HIV virus (AIDS)."

National Statistics

> -- 30-46% of all children are sexually assaulted in some way by the age of 18.
> -- 85% of the offenders are known to be an acquaintance or family member.
> -- 50% of all assaults take place in the home.
> -- Sexual assault cases involving boys are less likely to be reported, but recent research indicates they may be equally as at risk as girls.
> -- The National Women's Study survey estimates that 1 in 8 women have suffered some form of rape and that over 20% of all females have been raped or attacked.

(Courtesy of the Colorado Department of Health)

Suicide

The growing number of teenage suicides on Job Corps centers has contributed to a number of student dropouts and terminations even though the total number of successful suicides has remained the same over the years. The overall number of attempts has been climbing at an alarming rate. The students who are the most vulnerable are the orientation ones, those new students who have been at the center for only one to six months. An RA's worst fears come true when a student commits (or attempts to commit) suicide. Here are some warning signs that a student may be suicidal, according to the American Academy of Child and Adolescent Psychiatry.

1. Changes in eating and sleeping habits.
2. Withdrawal from friends, family and activities.
3. Violent or rebellious behavior; running away.
4. Drugs, alcohol abuse, changes in hygiene.
5. Persistent boredom, difficulty concentrating and decline in school work.
6. Inability to accept praise, feeling "rotten" inside.
7. Giving away favorite possessions.

Here are some warning signs that parents and Job Corps staff should look for additionally.

1. If a student's boy or girl friend on/off center or back home dumps him/her.
2. Receiving bad news from home. (Most of the time, the only way a student can get a ride home is to be terminated because Job Corps will not send a student home unless he has a death in the immediate family -- grandparent, parent, sibling).
3. Not reporting to the dormitory at the time required.
4. Missing from center for two or more days.

5. The reading, collecting and playing of the following products: Tarot cards, science fiction books, demonic jewelry or tattoos, dungeons and dragons games.

6. A tattoo can sometimes tell you a student's whole story - - lookout for new ones.

There have been an increasing number of students with mental health problems. More boys than girls seem to have problems mentally. But that could be because there are four times more male students at the Clearfield Job Corps center. The number of students with mental problems is usually more than the on-call psychologist can handle. As an RA, I was informed by my superior that Job Corps centers aren't designed to handle mentally distraught students, so I should just write their behavior up and hope we can get them terminated before they do harm to themselves or others. The counselors, RAs and teaching staff try their best to help the problem students, but they don't have the expertise to handle the complex problems of the mind.

AIDS

As of August 1989, all Job Corps centers across the nation will be required to retain HIV infected (seropositive) corps members on their centers according to specific criteria and guidelines as mandated by the national offices of the Job Corps. The students with the HIV virus do not have AIDS but do have the potential to spread AIDS through sexual contact. Contact, whether heterosexually, homosexually, bisexually or through IV drug users (addicts) are all dangerous if safe sex is not practiced and clean needles are not used when interacting. The progress and status of all AIDS infected students on the Job Corps centers are supposed to be closely monitored by the health maintenance team. The team consists of the following center individuals:

1. Center director or deputy director
2. Center physician and mental consultant
3. Manager and supervisor of health and nursing services
4. Manager or assistant manager of counseling

This team makes up less than three percent of the center staff and it is responsible for insuring that all HIV infected students at the center adhere to the specific guidelines of Job Corps policy or they will be terminated from the program. But by that time it's too late because of the way the kids run around with a different lover every week. One infected student could easily spread the AIDS virus to as many as 25 students in as few as six months, which is the average stay of most of the students. The other 98% of the center staff is not informed at all of a student's physical or mental condition, but they are required to handle all the students the same as if they have HIV. Here is a list of the staff the students trust and confide in when they need help or a friend to lend an ear, in the order of their importance.

1. Residential Advisor (RA)
2. Trade Teacher
3. Counselors
4. Security
5. Administration

Job Corps Students and the Law

Fugitives

Over the past 25 years of Job Corps' existence, law enforcement agencies have uncovered a number of fugitives. Felons on probation have been found hiding out waiting in Job Corps centers until the heat is off before returning to the areas from which they came or remaining in the surrounding communities. Some of them have been wanted on very dangerous and serious crimes.

Gang Related

Mothers, sending your kids to Job Corps to escape the gang problem doesn't work for the following reasons. The gangs are using the Job Corps program and its over 100 centers as a place to recruit new members, as well as setting up new locations in the surrounding communities to continue the business of drugs, extortion and prostitution. In fact, the gang problem has spread through the help of JC. The gangs from the larger cities are encouraging their membership to enlist new members from rural areas and towns that surround most Job Corps centers. You will find there are gang problems plaguing all Job Corps centers and the communities and cities around them. Gangs on center are not much different than the ones on the street. Members can and often do carry all types of weapons, guns, knives, etc. Despite Job Corps' efforts to monitor the gangs' activities on center, they have little control off center. Off center student situations are usually handled by local law enforcement.

*****

'Start-up' gang of Job Corps students
to be tried in beating

by Mary Ann Lemon
Standard-Examiner Davis Bureau

CLEARFIELD -- Six members of a "start-up" gang at the Clearfield Job Corps Center face trial Sept. 18 on charges of simple assault for allegedly beating a student who refused to join the gang, police and Job Corps official said.

The 18-year-old male student was thrown to the ground, beaten and kicked by a group of eight other Job Corps members early Aug. 27, said Clearfield Police Detective Tony Reyna.

The victim, who was bruised but not seriously injured, notified Job Corps authorities, and the eight were arrested Tuesday night and booked into the Davis County Jail, Reyna said.

Reyna described the students as would-be gang members who wanted to start a gang at the center. One student had been affiliated with an East Coast gang called the Black Gangster Disciples, but otherwise the group was not part of an organized gang, he said.

"We believe these were newer kids who were new to the area and new to the system and were trying to test what they could do," Reyna said.

Job Corps Center Director John Crosby said any students involved in the alleged beating incident would be expelled from the center and sent home.

"No matter what happens, they're not coming back here," he said.

Crosby said many Job Corps students come to the Clearfield program from big cities where gangs are a part of life. He said gang activity is not tolerated at the center.

"A lot of kids had gang affiliations -- it's the only way you can survive in the places they come from. Most of them leave it behind them when they come here, but sometimes it flares up," he said.

Facing trial in 2nd Circuit Court on Class B misdemeanor charges of simple assault are:

Robert Jamision, 21; Walter Surveyer, 21; William Morgan, 20; Kenneth Duarte, 20; Arthur Leroy Marcotte, 22; and Mickey Joe Combs, 19.

The seventh and eighth suspects, both juveniles, were taken to MOWEDA Youth Home in Roy.

*****

Homicide, rape, robbery, burglary, auto theft, arson and aggravated assault have risen drastically in the communities around a number of the larger Job Corps centers.

Riots

Gang banging, fighting between students, gangs, races, trade groups, and residential dormitories are as common on large Job Corps campuses as a bad meal. The handling of riot situations by the Job Corps management is usually mass termination of the students from the program. Assault, extortion and robbery are tools of the trade and are commonly used by bigger, more aggressive students and gangs. They will try to intimidate the smaller, less physical students by threatening to do bodily harm or by constant harassment. The bullies are usually associated or accompanied by a large or small gang numbering from two to twenty within their dormitories. At times the gangs may take control of the dorm and even have positions of authority within the dorm and center campuses. Once gang members have a little power on center they become a real threat to the other students. As with many gangs, the leader or leadership is usually bigger and much stronger and older than the followers.

*****

Clearfield Job Corps riot quelled
by Kristine M. Loosley and Tim Gurrister
Standard-Examiner Staff

CLEARFIELD -- A fight erupted into what police and eyewitnesses called "a riot" on the campus of the Clearfield Job Corps Center late Saturday.

Nearly 30 police cruisers from CLearfield, Layton and neighboring cities raced onto the Clearfield campus at about 10:30 p.m. with light and sirens on after a call went out over police radio channels describing a riot in progress.

Police later called for additional backup, including police dogs. Radio dispatchers referred to the incident as a riot in calling for help.

"There's a big fight going on, that's all I know," a security officer at the gate of the Antelope Drive entrance to the center told a reporter. "I can't let anyone back there."

Davis County Sheriff Glenn Clary said he'd been advised at 10:45 that "a couple hundred kids were causing some problems at the Job Corps."

Clary said Clearfield had asked for assistance from other agencies to handle what appeared to be "a semi-riot type thing" that had started during a large gathering of Job Corps students in an auditorium.

37

He said he didn't have details. The sheriff's office was acting as backup assistance to Clearfield police, he said.

Two students who said they witnessed the fight breaking out came running off campus just before 10:30 p.m., saying they wanted to get away from the trouble to avoid being caught up in it.

"There's a huge fight in there, man," said one student, who would not give his name. He said the fight started between just a few students and escalated until more than 200 were involved.

Fighting students filled the mall in front of the student dormitories, said the eyewitnesses. They said they saw no weapons.

The Clearfield Job Corps, established in 1966, is a residence school that offers vocational training programs to students who have had problems completing traditional high school courses. Students are recruited from several states.

The fight appeared to be between students who had been at the center for some time and a new group that arrived Tuesday from St. Louis, the eyewitnesses said.

*****

Riot revised to fight, 3 are arrested

CLEARFIELD -- Three adult students from the CLearfield Job Corps Center were arrested following a Saturday night fracas at the center that was quelled by officers from throughout northern Davis County.

Originally called a riot by police dispatchers when cares were being called out shortly after 10:25 p.m. Saturday, it was described Sunday in a Clearfield Police news release as "a couple of people fighting" surrounded by a lot of onlookers.

Clearfield Police said there were no serious injuries during the melee, and credited that to the volume and quickness of response by area police officers.

The three men who were arrested are being held in the Davis County Jail.

Officers from Clearfield, Centerville, Kaysville, Sunset, Clinton and Layton along with the Davis County Sheriff's Office and the Utah Highway Patrol all responded to the scene backing up Job Corps security, a Clearfield dispatcher said.

Witnesses said Saturday night that the fight appeared to be between some students who had been at the center for some time and a new group that arrived early last week from St. Louis.

Job Corps is a residential vocational training program that recruits students from around the United States.

Clearfield Police said that an investigation into the matter is continuing, but could not say if additional arrests would be made.

*****

The Big Fight

Riots like this one printed in a local newspaper have been happening throughout Job Corps' existence. In the past ten years, riots have become more frequent, violent and deadly.

Negative news articles are usually downplayed by the local newspapers the next day. A number of towns and cities that have Job Corps centers are hurting economically and are doing everything possible to keep people working and their towns financially alive.

Over 25 years have passed with communities having to have the Job Corps program forced down their throats and not being able to do anything about it. They are now finding it very difficult to do without the federal tax dollars Job Corps provides. Negative publicity about a business nowadays is usually all it takes to send a company packing. So too, their fears of losing their economic base have forced a number of these community newspapers to withhold or alter all negative publicity about local businesses and federal programs, so it doesn't reach the national level.

Vietnamese/Asian

Their numbers are few but their unity is great. They communicate as one. Most of the time they do not start trouble, but they often come together to fend off the attacker or attackers. They eat, sleep sometimes two or more in the same bed. This is not an uncommon sight. They often have a problem speaking the English language and are frequently found speaking in their native language. They are very respectful to adults and people in authority. They are a quiet group when communicating with others outside their race or sect (gang). They often show more self restraint than other gangs on center.

Indian/Native American

Pueblo, Ute, Navajo, Apache and Crow are just a few of the Indian tribes. The Indian culture, tradition and religion are completely ignored by most of the centers. The majority of the Indians enrolled in Job Corps centers are entering with a heavy dependence on alcohol (liquor, firewater). One student told me he had been drinking since he was six years old and that on his reservation there are more liquor stores than grocery markets. Also, his whole family is alcoholics. The Indians usually stay the shortest time of all the enrollees, mostly because of their alcohol dependence. The life and treatment they received on the reservation sometimes makes it difficult for them to contend with the rules and white people. They are lovers of the great outdoors and freedom, and they will fight to remain so.

White/European American

Like the black and hispanic gangs, the white gang members are just as troublesome, but unlike their counterparts, white gangs only account for a small percentage of the white students. White gangs are made up predominantly of whites and base their groups on remaining racially segregated. They often act superior and treat others outside their race as being inferior human beings. Members will often place themselves into positions of authority on center like jaycheckers, dormitory officers, etc. They often have tattoos of German Swastikas, upside down crucifixes and medallions. A number of them may belong to the Ku Klux Klan or Neo-Nazi movements.

Black/African American

These gangs are usually from the largest cities in the U.S. where there is a lot of crime, drugs, drive by killings, etc. They will try to intimidate other students with the use of body language involving facial and hand gestures. They prefer working and associating with members of there sect (gang). Very seldom do they fight alone. The Bloods and Crips from California are two of the many.

Mexican/Hispanic American

These gangs are mostly from the western U.S. including California, Nevada, Texas and Colorado, though they may also be from New York. All claim to have gang problems in their hispanic communities. They will frequently have conversations in the Spanish language. They also prefer working and associating with members of the gang from back home. Out of all the other ethnic cultures they seem to better relate and socialize with the black students, and it is not uncommon for them to be of the same sect (gang). They also will use body language in the form of facial and hand gestures as a form of intimidation. They frequently carry knives or shives (sharpened piece of metal four to six inches or longer). They often show little restraint when confronted by people of authority, other students and police officers. Women are also recruited as gang members and back home frequently dress themselves and their children in the gang colors.

Homosexual

These gangs are a reality. Their numbers are very few at times but they have no fear of the other gangs or students. In fact, I have noticed that in a strange way the other students have learned to communicate with and respect homosexual students, mostly, I believe, for their fighting abilities. Job Corps' open environment and the fact that the male students outnumber the female students throughout the Job Corps program five to one helps the homosexual population to thrive.

A Word of Caution

To associate yourself with gangs and their negative activity usually results in situations that could lead to your termination from center, a jail term, serious bodily harm or, worse, your death. Some signals to look out for that just may help you to identify the dreaded gang member are tattoos, medallions, LA Raiders clothing, colors of their clothing, the way they wear their hats and their use of hand signals.

My warning to the parents -- the gangs of today are forever changing. They may look and talk differently throughout the times, but their outlook on life remains the same: "Why should I worry about tomorrow when today is but half over?"

Higher Education

I have noticed a number of students entering Job Corps today are entering with their high school diplomas and with the promise of going to college. A small number of the students can and do get the opportunity to go to local colleges in the surrounding communities outside the centers, but not all centers offer the college program. Also, they may require you to wait six months on center before entering the college program. I have found that a number of students were misled. They received assurances that as soon as they arrived they could start college but upon their arrival they were informed it wasn't to be until six months' time had passed. In the mean time, they would have to take up a trade. Of the students who enter the college program, very few ever stay long enough to finish.

If your children are under 18 years of age, I recommend you keep them at home until they become so. The Job Corps recruiters will and frequently do enroll kids promising all types of trades, but once a kid arrives, he may be informed he cannot participate in a number of trades since he is under the age limit. I have calculated the dropout rate to be five to one, but that's nothing when compared to the placement rate. Only about 1 in 400 students will be placed in full time employment.

Students' Complaints about Conditions

The Food

Most of the students refuse to eat the food because they say it contains too much grease or it is never cooked all the way through. Almost all the oriental students never eat in the cafeteria because the food makes them sick. Most of them have hot plates, or hot pots and are often found cooking in their rooms -- something that is not allowed, can be very dangerous and has been known to cause fires in the past. Some of the sensitive students and the newer ones tend to suffer allergic reactions.

Deteriorating health, depression, homesickness, fear, abuses from other students and staff contribute to the outstanding number of kids who never complete the Job Corps programs. Students also mention unheated rooms, cold floors and discrimination. Women in some of the large Job Corps centers go through hell. Pranks are played on incoming and outgoing students.

Disease Problems

When a contagious disease is found on center it is usually too late to inform the surrounding communities. And it's not the best thing to do from a management point of view, since it could cause a panic in their bank account.

Classes Too Large

Some of the centers have the same problem as some of our country's lower class inner city schools: too many students in a classroom and not enough teachers. But this problem is not the doing of the taxpayer or poor living and unemployment conditions like back home. It is caused solely by the contractors and their greed. Large class sizes with fewer teachers equals more money for the investors.

Fighting

Most of the large Job Corps centers have a boxing program. Students who wish to fight can learn to fight for sport

and fun. The total number of boxing exhibition fights held in the
gymnasiums of all Job Corps centers for a year couldn't equal one
season of the total number of attacks, fights and assaults that go
on throughout the second largest center.

Education

The trade classes are full of gang members nowadays, and
a number of students show up just to sleep off a hangover from
the night before, which seems to go over just fine with the trade
instructors. Their main concern is that the students keep a
physical presence in the classroom.

Let me say that with 1500 plus students on the Clearfield
Job Corps center, there is a fight or an argument an average of
about every three minutes. The most dangerous form of violence
on Job Corps centers are student attacks on other students. Many
of the students in the Job Corps program complain mostly about
the violence on center.

There is no question that non-collected violence on and
off Job Corps centers is on the rise. It has been since the 1970s.
When there's a fight involving a large number of students, the
director of the center will order a lock down. No one is allowed
to depart from the center grounds without orders from the
directors. Lock downs have been known to last from three to
eight hours.

Arrests and Homicides

Job Corps Turns Out Pros -- But Some Say Cons, Too

by Chris Jorgensen
The Salt Lake Tribune

When a 19-year-old man was shot in the back last week on a crowded sidewalk in downtown Salt Lake City, police already knew the script.

The confessed shooter, Antwon Warren, was a gang leader who moved to Utah from St. Louis. He also once was enrolled in Job Corps, a vocational trade school at Clearfield that gives 1,300 young adults from around the country a chance to break out of poverty.

Warren, 19, miserably failed the federal program and was immediately shipped back to Missouri. But like many other Clearfield Job Corps dropouts, Warren returned to Utah, a state so vulnerable to gang recruiting it has earned the label "The Big Easy."

Eight days before the shooting, Warren was arrested in Salt Lake CIty with a stolen car. He also was in possession of two guns and nearly 300 rounds of ammunition.

The Main Street shooting, investigators said, started outside Crossroads Plaza with a fistfight between members of the Crenshaw Mafia Gangsters (CMG) and the Tongan Crip Gangsters (TCG), rival gangs. It ended when Warren, a "CMG," shot 19-year-old Antone Mataele, a "TGC." Warren was five feet from the victim when he fired a single round from his .25-caliber, chrome-plate d pistol.

Police -- and many northern Utah residents -- say brazen gunplay is typical of the trouble some Job Corps students bring with them.

"Society screwed up these kids," said Layton police Sgt. Rex Brimhall. "Somewhere society has to accept responsibility for them....Kids do benefit from Job Corps. Unfortunately, the byproduct of that is the crap we have to put up with."

Job Corps officials say the cops are exaggerating. They claim the number of Job Corps students committing crimes in Utah is only a fraction of the crimes committed by the state's young adults.

"It's so convenient for police to blame their problems on us," fumes Sandra Kinji, a Job Corps outreach administrator. "It's another way for police to ignore what's going on in their own cities. It's a generalization and I'm tired of it."

During the past 12 years, at least five homicides have been committed on the Wasatch Front by current or former Job Corps students. One occurred on the school's 83-acre campus in 1985 when a student was stabbed to death after being wrongly accused of a theft.

Assaults are common. Since January, Clearfield police have made more than 70 arrests on the campus alone.

Every weekend, busloads of students are dropped off at Job Corps-operated "hospitality centers" in Ogden and Salt Lake City. At least 28 armed off-duty police officers, who call each other "cattle ranchers," are on the Job Corps payroll to keep students in line while on weekend leaves.

Officers from both cities joke about charting the next crime wave by what time the blue Job Corps bus pulls into town. It's not entirely a joke. One deputy Davis County prosecutor said a day rarely passes without a Job Corps student on the docket.

On the other hand, most students at Job Corps stay out of trouble, graduate, land jobs and go on to lead productive lives. They go from being on welfare to being taxpayers, Ms. Kinji said. "The Corps speaks for itself. We're completely misunderstood and we're the best in the business for low-income kids."

The clearfield Job Corps is the third largest of the nations's 108 Job Corps centers, employs 485 staff members and teaches 19 trades. It has a $21 million federal budget, most of which is spent locally, Ms. Kinji points out. About 300 of the Clearfield students are women, some of them mothers. About 40 percent are minorities.

Nationwide, taxpayers spend $920 million to train some 62,000 students at the Job Corps centers.

The Gang Issue

Gangs and Job Corps have become synonymous in the minds of several Wasatch Front police departments. Many claim they can trace the roots of Utah's most violent gangs to youths brought here by Job Corps.

Police point to the case of Gary Nicolas Avila, known on the streets of Salt Lake County as "Baby Face." Avila came to the Clearfield Job Corps Center from California in the late 1980s, but was swiftly expelled and sent home.

Within months, he relocated to Salt Lake City, where he immediately began recruiting kids for his "Surenos 13" gang. An armed-robbery conviction landed him in prison and he later was paroled to Oxnard Calif. Even in his absence, the gang members he recruited continue to terrorize Utah residents and businesses.

Felon Dumping

Last January, 29-year-old Bill Terry of South Ogden pulled into a convenience store in Clearfield at 3 a.m. It was directly across the street from the Job Corps Center.

As Mr. Terry climbed back into his car after buying something to eat, he was stabbed in the chest and shoulder by two Job Corps students who were tired of waiting for a bus and wanted his car.

Until that morning, Mr. Terry had never been the victim of a crime.

"And then I run into these punks who I guess were brought here from California," he said. "We've got our own troubles with kids and crime in Utah without bringing bad kids here."

Critics call bringing troubled teenagers to Utah "felon dumping." A few cases stand out:

-- In 1977, 20-year-old David Defoe shot his Ogden housemate Carl McIntosh in the mouth and then forged two of the 67-year-old victim's personal checks. Witnesses testified Defoe had been ordered to the Utah Job Corps from Kansas after he confessed to shooting his mother and stuffing her body into trash bags.

-- Mark Deron Harrison, 19, was sent to Clearfield Job Corps from Missouri in 1989. In April of that year, he shot a 22-year-old Air Force airman in the eye outside a Salt Lake City bar after the victim had bumped Harrison's girlfriend on the dance floor.

Nationally, youths at several of the Job Corps locations have clashed with the law. But Job Corps supporters say those isolated disasters distract the public from the program's successes.

More criminals are lured to Salt Lake and other urban areas by new businesses, area universities and the military than by Job Corps, says Mr. Spergel of the University of Chicago.

And despite "a couple of bad apples," Sen. Orrin Hatch, among many, remains an adamant Job Corps defender. The ax nearly fell on Job Corps when president Ronald Reagan complained that the annual cost per student -- now $14,000 -- rivaled tuition at Harvard.

*****

Job Corps says policy cuts arrests

by James Nickerson
Standard-Examiner Davis Bureau

CLEARFIELD -- Policies designed to curb misconduct at the Clearfield Job Corps have decreased off-center student arrests by two-thirds since they were implemented last year, officials say.

Strict "no tolerance" policies have been in place since October 1991 when center Director John Crosby declared "war" on gang members and the illegal use of drugs and alcohol by Job Corps students.

As a result, 72 students suspected of either gang-related activity or illegal drug use and alcohol abuse were expelled.

Until the policy was enacted, off-center arrests of students averaged more than 34 a month. Now the average has dropped to 10 a month.

Nearly 1,500 student attend the government job training facility for people 16-21.

48

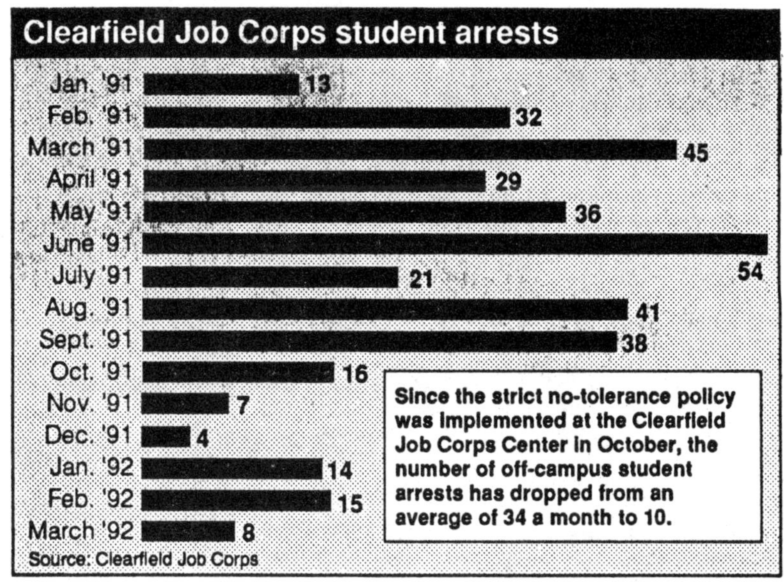

Standard-Examiner

"We told them we can't have them drinking and creating problems, because they are guests in this community," he said. "They have taken that to heart. The warning is given during orientation, and then if they are in violation of the policy they're gone."

In the five months before the policy was in force, Clearfield and Layton police reported 111 arrests of Job Corps students, but five months since the policy, the two cities have arrested 30 students.

"The problems have not gone away and probably never will, but they have gone down," said Layton Police Chief Doyle Talbot.

Clearfield Police Inspector Bill Holthaus said the key to the Job Corps policy is that it is tougher than state law.

"Students -- even those who were of age -- used to go buy alcohol and get drunk and do stupid things," he said. "But now they can't. It's not a violation of state law, but it is a violation of Job Corps policy, and you've got to give them credit for that."

Holthaus said the combination of supervision and enforcement makes the policies work.

"They are using shuttle buses to take kids into town now, and they are sending people home when they violate policies," he said. "They have taken a very pro-active approach to the problems that were there and you can see the difference,"

Crosby said being consistent with the policy is the key to giving it teeth.

"You have got to stick with the policy no matter whether it's the best student on campus or the worst," Crosby said.

Crosby said the average stay of students has been lengthened by 30 days since things have quieted down. It normally takes students 18 months to two years to complete a trade, although some leave early for various reasons.

"There was a sense of uneasiness before" the no-tolerance policy, Crosby said. "People were drinking and nobody wanted to be around them."

Crosby said he is hopeful that the bad rap he said the Job Corps gets from the news media will cease now that order has been restored.

"I have to be optimistic that the more good things we do and the fewer bad things, the intelligent people will see the good things going on here," he said. "It will take some time."

Different Points of View

Ron Garfield, Manager of a Large Apartment Complex

"Well, I don't know a whole lot about the operation of things out at Job Corps. All I know about is what I see come here after completing the program: kids looking for a place to stay, so I give them an apartment. We have some of the lowest prices in town on one and two bedroom apartment rentals. But even at our low price, 90 percent of the kids that come here don't make it.

"My wife and I try t help them out as much as we can. They come here with nothing -- no car, furniture, family or job. If we have tenants move out who don't need or are selling their furniture, we let the kids (ex-Job Corps students) know about it. But for the most part, they are sleeping on the floor right up to the day they leave without paying their rent.

"My wife and I have been running this place for about eight years now and when we first started, the owner filled us in on the problem areas. He said the last manager he had running the apartments had a real problem with people not paying their rent on time and moving out without notice. But now thcy pay their rent one month in advance. We try to handle them with a firm but Christian hand when we start to see the bottom start to fall out from under them.

"A number of them are good kids, so we try to work with them. They start out just fine. Most of them usually have money to pay for about two months' rent, but after that first month, a number of them start having problems from not being able to cope with living on their own, not being able to find a job, or losing a job. To get by, they will start having rent parties, inviting their friends from Job Corps and whoever else they happen to meet on the street. They drink and do drugs until late at night. A number of times I had to call the police to stop fights and things like that.

"I got this kid named Milton who's been here for about four months. He has a job working for Minit Lube for minimum wage. He has certificates, honors and achievement awards for professional excellence for completing the automotive and heavy truck repair at the top of his class at Job Corps, but the only job that they could find him was part time at a lube place. You would figure with that training he would have gotten one of those high-paying union jobs.

"Milton is a pretty good kid for 23, but lately he's been having problems with his girlfriend. She's a lot older than he is and I think she has three kids. One day I received a phone call from the tenant directly under his apartment complaining about loud arguing and fighting going on in the apartment above her - - Milton's place. I let him know that if I received more complaints he would have to move out. Don't they teach them how to get along with life on the outside?"

Mr. Tucker, Residential Advisor/Inspector
"When I first hired on back in June of 1978, Thiokol was the corporation that controlled the Clearfield Job Corps Center. They only had four units. Boy, things were a lot different than now. I worked graveyard for about five years. I remember we didn't have any really formal training. Sometimes we would cover two dorms a piece at night. Quite a number of times there would be a problem in another dorm, like fights or something, and I would have to leave the dorm to help the dorm that was having the problem, leaving my dorm unattended.

"I was an RA in group life for about nine years and then I became an inspector. When I started back in '78 the dorms were about 80 percent black and then later on it started to dwindle down to 60, 70 and then 50 percent. I remember when they came in with the Cubes. When the Cubes first came they called them boat people. They brought about 50 of them. Quite a few of them had bolo knives and stuff like that on them. There were a lot of problems with the Cubes because they really didn't understand the American way, plus the procedures and programs of Job Corps, and that was when Thiokol was managing the center. Later on after the 1980s, they started recruiting larger numbers of other races like Laotians, Vietnamese and rural whites.

"Things were a lot better as far as morale, pay of the staff and overall treatment of the students when Thiokol was running the center. Things changed a lot when MTC (Management and Training Corporation) got the contract to run the center. They cut the staff's yearly performance bonuses, the discipline of the students started changing with the hiring of different directors, the activities of the students started declining. Many times I worked a dorm with 80 or more students when it was meant for 60. We never had any staff to cover the dorms. In most cases I think Job Corps had fulfilled their contracts between themselves and the students who enrolled into the program.

"In the past year (1991-92) I have seen larger numbers of black kids sent home, terminated for the same offense as their white counterparts who were not terminated. In some cases the black students may have been a little more aggressive than the others, but they could have been a little more patient with them. Also, in some cases, there may have been a lack of communication between the black students and the staff, especially the white staff.

"I have seen students sent to jail because of falsehoods, such as the case where a girl stated a young fellow molested her. The young fellow, coming from another part of the country wasn't used to being around that type of student and what really happened was that the white girl tried to put herself off on the young man and when he didn't go along with the program, she claimed he molested her and said things to her. This caused the young man to be put in jail. When the problem came before the Standard Review Board, we found out she had a history of this kind of behavior. Further investigation by the review board found that the young man was innocent and he was able to finish the program.

"Some security people were quite aggressive in dealing with the students. Instead of talking to the students, they would use physical force in front of the other students, causing the other students to go off. There was some bias, some problems. I would say we had about a 60 percent turnover in staff because management did not know how to deal or communicate with them. The high turnover in staff resulted in students putting in for transfers to other centers or terminating.

"Some of the staff did not know how to deal with the students because they lacked compassion, understanding, and then you had some women who were working the dorms who were, I would say, too motherly. In other words, they were too soft in dealing with students. Students really took advantage of them. They would manipulate them. They did what they wanted in the dorm, causing a lot of confusion and fights in their dealings such as loansharking, selling noodles, candy, cakes, drugs, etc.

"In one instance a bus came in and the students saw a dog out by the security gate and I guess they thought the dog was there to look for drugs, etc., so the students started piling the drugs or whatever they had and began throwing it out the window.

"I remember one time a college professor from a university came down and hired on as an RA and said he wanted to see what it would be like. After only one day of work, he resigned and on his way out the gate he said to give his pay to the students because he couldn't handle it. You see, his academic training in psychology is an altogether different type of training from what I dealt with out on the center. You cannot input total academic training into that atmosphere because it's totally different. You have to correlate academics and common sense and street stuff in that type of environment.

"You see, an RA has to instill into them the fact that other students will try to find out if they are weak or strong. You have to instill in them the importance of personal hygiene and working together in total harmony. Sometimes we get students who come straight from a mental institution and we have to weed them out. We'd start the paperwork for getting them out because you could tell there was something wrong with them because of their behavior.

"Another time, another RA and I were working together for once in the same dorm on the graveyard shift and a drunk student gave us a hard time out on the ramp. He refused to tell us what dorm he was in, and he went on to tell us that we had nothing to do with him, that we could not tell him anything because he was a student staff member. He went on to tell us that he would have our jobs. This type of activity from him went on for a few days. We wrote out negative reports on him, but nothing was done. Then one night the unit coordinator said he was missing some students out of a dorm. I told him I thought I knew where one of the students was, so we went from H Dorm to F Dorm and came in the back door. That was where we found the student in a compromising homosexual position. This was the student who had been coming in drunk. The other student was a minor, age 16. The outcome of it all was the two students went to jail. When they went to court the judge gave the older of the two, age 21, who pleaded guilty, three months in jail. The younger one was sent home."

Edward Smith, Residential Advisor

"Strong students survive and those students who are not so strong tend to have more problems. In any kind of training or residential-type program you are going to experience some type of problem with personality conflicts between individual students, groups and geographic make-up.

"As far as specific incidents, I would say in the past four or so years the program seems to have done more for the quality of life of the student population, such as dorm enhancement and that type of thing. When I first started out there five years ago, it was not as attractive as it is now. They dumped a lot of money into the facility and a lot of it went toward self-help projects. We'd get a bunch of people and get a lot of labor accomplished all in the name of learning.

"I guess one of the things they could have done better to enhance the program is to follow up on their placement programs, maybe double the staff of the placement people, because one of the concerns of the student population is, "Now I have this training, but not a whole lot of placement opportunities." Also, there seems to have been some selective racism in the placement of the students. It might be kept quiet, but in working with the students in a residential setting you learn about it. There's absolutely racism involved in the job training because I've seen students of color denied or selectively placed in other trades rather than the trade of their choice. I've had students complete the trade they were put in initially and still have difficulty getting into the trade of their choice, so don't tell me racism isn't alive and well at Job Corps because I know it is. There have been a couple of times I was about to go to bat for some students because of that in particular.

"When you talk about some of the crimes committed there, yeah, because we're dealing with the population out there. A large number of them have had some scrape with the law and have been directed to Job Corps. There're a lot of crimes that go unreported, just like in the private sector.

"The success rate of completion for locals is like 50-50. Their stay could be one day to one year, but we try to get them through in a 90 day period.

"The morale among the staff has been very low, mostly because the periodic cost of living increase is nothing when compared to the amount of profit the company (MTC) is making. You would think that one so rich would be more generous to those down in the lower echelons to afford them better living arrangements.

"When an incident happens, people have a tendency not to volunteer information for fear or reprisals from other students. Sometimes there are those who don't have the tools of the English language to be able to construct a statement that is descriptive enough of the incident.

"I think the entire screening process should be overhauled because the recruiters mislead students in order to get the body count. They show pictures and brochures that are misrepresentative of the facility they are going to. The recruiters are in for the money -- body count -- like I said. The more bodies there are, the more money they get to count.

"I've heard of female prostitution out there, but not male prostitution. It seems like there is a direct correlation between the amount of crime in the community and the number of students going into town. With any gathering of young people, there is a tendency to go along with the crowd (gang) or the

popular ideas, or peer pressure, that is quite influential out there
(Job Corps).

"Alcohol and drug experimentation is alive and well out
there and I've done paperwork on many incidents of alcohol and
drug use.

"On student paydays, perhaps teaching skills of money
management or independent living, social skills -- although they
say it's taught -- more emphasis should be put on these types of
problem areas. Some of the students start out on $40 per month -
- $18 every two and a half weeks or so -- and when you get some
of those slicksters, straight up people who are used to having
grand theft dealt with, that's no money at all. I think the expe-
dient elimination of problem individuals after receiving negative
reports on them would be a good idea because sometimes it
causes problems when they are allowed to stay. They go on to
cause additional problems, and I think this is in direct relation to
the fact that keeping the individual there longer means more
money is made. I don't think the profit obtained is worth the
emotional trauma to some of having a bad student administra-
tively held on the rolls. It doesn't do anything to the morale of
either the student or staff populations in the direct line of those
students."

Anthony Thompson, Ex-Student/Welder

I was happy to receive the opportunity to speak to the
June '92 graduating class on how I was doing eight years after Job
Corps. I look back and remember my first day in Job Corps
(Clearfield). It was January 6, 1982. I went there with the
intention of completing a trade and high school. In between my
arrival and my completion was a total of 26 months. I was young
and not serious about life. I had a real bad attitude. I was still into
the outdoor life such as drinking, smoking, drugs and fighting. I've
done things that if I wasn't in Job Corps I would have more than
likely gone to jail.

"Now don't get me wrong, not every kid at Job Corps was
like me -- wild. I can only speak for myself. Being in Job Corps
was like being institutionalized. You have people to look out and

watch over you. I didn't take life seriously until certain people stood up for me when I got in trouble and was about to get kicked out of the program. A counselor by the name of Mr. Tucker became a father figure to me and many of the others; Dave Crittendon believed in me and gave me a second chance when Job Corps was about to terminate me.

"After that I buckled down, went to class and received my High School Diploma and a trade in welding. I even made student of the month.

"When I got out of Job Corps, it was like starting all over again. I got in with the wrong crowd, drinking and smoking dope. I was evicted three times from my apartment and started to have seizures from drug use. Not until I checked into Alcoholics Anonymous and found Christ did I change.

"I look back at Job Corps and proudly say, 'Thanks for giving me a chance.' Now I tell people I meet that Job Corps is not so bad. Just like human beings, it has its faults as well, but just as human beings can stand for change, so can Job Corps."

Senator Orrin Hatch (R-Utah), Committee on Labor
and Human Resources (Chairperson)

Before I was elected to the U.S. Senate in 1976, most of what I had heard about Job Corps depicted it as just another "Great Society" program born during the Johnson administration, along with a host of other Santa Claus programs. It is no secret that I have never believed in "handouts" from the government. Such public sector programs have proven ineffective in addressing the *causes* of poverty; they have only helped to perpetuate it at taxpayers' expense. Our national network of private, proprietary and non-profit civic organizations, on the other hand, have a proven track record. Such programs as the United Way, Catholic Community Services, Salvation Army, the LDS Bishops' Storehouse and thousands of local groups across the country are evidence of America's caring for those in need.

Conversely, income maintenance programs administered by government tend to inspire permanent dependence on them. The Job Corps, I thought, was not more than a handout for youth so we could start their welfare dependence much earlier in life, in keeping with the cradle-to-grave paternalism the federal government was practicing in the 1960s. After taking office as a Senator from Utah, and my assignment on the Labor and Human Resources Committee, I began to learn much more about the Job Corps program. I studied most of the reports on the effectiveness of the program and the long-term success of the students.

Perhaps most importantly, I was invited to visit the Clearfield Job Corps Center in my home state of Utah that was operated by Management and Training Corporation. I was greatly impressed by what I saw and the enthusiastic responses of the students. It was clear that the Job Corps was not a handout program at all, but a hand-up program designed to give youth the chance to learn lifetime skills.

The Job Corps is a unique concept for providing skills training and job counseling primarily to disadvantaged youth: 85 percent are high school dropouts and 100 percent are below the poverty level. As many as 25 percent have been rejected by the U.S. Armed Forces due to their inability to meet the minimum entrance requirements. The individual Job Corps centers, managed and operated by public and private organizations, concentrate on developing competency in the basic educational skills and providing the training required for employment in the private sector or acceptance into the military.

The training programs have been designed by individual centers, in close collaboration with business and labor unions. The basic Job Corps programs are recognized for their effectiveness in not only basic education and general training, but in changing the attitudes of formerly-discouraged young people. The private sector's faith in the Job Corps is exhibited by its willingness to be involved in the operation of Job Corps centers or in launching and career development opportunities. Further, Job Corps centers are residential and provide students with the kind of support that accrues from having nutritious meals, health services, student government, organized sports and recreation, and the chance to see life in a positive atmosphere.

This unique concept is one through which teenagers can develop some self-discipline, respect for others, respect for authority, and can receive the friendship and support of their fellow students. Counselors are equipped to handle personal problems. Students can become well-rounded, productive individuals able to cope with the day-to-day problems we all face and who can derive some self-satisfaction from having done so.

The success of the concept is clear from the statistics: In 1979, 93 percent of Job Corps' enrollees were placed either in private-sector jobs, admitted to school, or entered the Armed Forces. The placement rate of the Job Corps has increased steadily since it was created in 1964. Mathematician Policy Research, Inc., in a study performed for the Employment and Training Administration for the Department of Labor, found that:

1. Corpsmembers averaged over four weeks more employment per year than the control group.
2. Corpsmembers averaged approximately $500.00 more per year in earnings than the control group.
3. There was double the likelihood of entrance into the U.S. Armed Forces.
4. Corpsmembers averaged three fewer weeks of public assistance than the control group.
5. Five Percent of Corpsmembers went on to college, while none in the control group did.
6. Corpsmembers averaged one week less per year of unemployment insurance than the control group.
7. There were significant Job Corps-related effects in terms of reducing out-of-wedlock children among females.

Robert Taggart, in a study issued by W. E. Upjohn Institute for Employment Research, estimated the social benefit cost ratio of the Job Corps is about 45 to 1. His study is comprehensive since it includes such factors as reduced criminal activity, approximately $2,112.00 per Corpsmember; reduced treatment costs for drug and alcohol abuse, about $30.00 per corpsmember; reduced dependence on transfer payments, approximately $1,515.00 per Corpsmember; and most importantly, increased post-program output approximately $3,896.00 per Corpsmember.

In short, I support the Job Corps because it works. We can count the results, measured by those young people who become full, contributing members of our society, rather than welfare junkies.

Since becoming a strong supporter of the Job Corps program, I had the privilege of being asked to speak to the students of the Clearfield Center at their graduation. I felt a little like a proud parent, proud of the accomplishments of these determined young citizens. They worked hard for an education, for job skills and for self-respect. They beat the odds, and I know they will not give up if the going gets a little rough. They realize that nothing worth having is easily obtained, and that the fuel that drives all of us to greater effort is not the money, or power or applause.

These extrinsic rewards do not last. The payoff for these graduates is the personal satisfaction they feel from choosing right over expediency and from going the extra mile.

These young people are the future of our nation. The Job Corps is where they are learning they truly have a stake in it. While other welfare programs provide the bare necessities, and pretend to be compassionate even while the computer routinely processes and mails out checks, the Job Corps students understand that a better life requires a life of effort, and a pursuit of personal excellence.

Author's Note

For Senator Hatch, support of the Job Corps program truly came when MTC headquarters in Ogden, Utah, one of his major supporters, became the managing firm of the nation's second largest center with over a $20 million budget. Senator Hatch's support of the Job Corps program grew from that 1984 takeover of the Clearfield, Utah, Job Corps Center by MTC. It is estimated that MTC profited over $1 million that year from the takeover.

Also, Senator Hatch only states figures and statistics from outdated reports of little importance, based only on Job Corps' small number of placement figures, not total enrollment figures.

Life After Job Corps

Clay, age 22, described his experiences. "I was harassed about going to school when I already had my high school diploma. I couldn't see going to school for something I already had, so that's how it all started. They wanted to send me back through grade 8 and up. I thought I would be coming to Job Corps to take up training to be an RN, my first choice, or security or cooking. When I got there, the trade placement staff started to make me do things against my will. After that I said goodbye to the center and walked out. Two or three weeks later they called me up at my mom's place and started harassing her a little bit about my coming back. I explained to them the problems I was having with my trade, and they assured me everything would be okay if I went to another center.

"A few weeks later I was at another center, this one a lot smaller -- only 300 students. I took a trade in cooking because it was the only trade to fit my goals since I couldn't get in RN or security. People were getting terminated or phased out of the Job Corps center for reasons like the dress code. Raiders jackets and other Raider things are looked upon by the government or the government staff as being gang related. Right now they would terminate me because I have holes in my pants, or maybe for wearing this jacket and that leather cowboy hat I had on earlier. They would have terminated me for that. Disagreeing with the way things are run on center, arguments with staff members or another student gets you terminated -- lots of things like that. You're not free to express yourself like back home where you can walk anywhere, anyhow, dress anyway and talk to anybody you want. Up there you don't have that freedom.

"Now after seven months as a Job Corps member I was terminated for nothing. Now I have nowhere to go but here on the streets and those checks they were supposed to be handing out at the end of a student's stay in Job Corps aren't here. I've been out since October 18th and now its December 16th -- nothing. I've been staying at St. Ann's shelter waiting for my checks and the only place I can find work is at the dog food place for a few hours at a time, which doesn't pay much. There're a lot of students who have been terminated staying at the mission. Most of them go back to what they were doing or start selling drugs or look for work through temporary services.

"When I was recruited my recruiter said there were a lot of jobs to be trained in for good pay and stuff, with the training allowance ranging anywhere from $50.00 to $100.00 every two weeks. Then I found it wasn't true. Medical benefits are another example. They say Job Corps will pay all your expenses, even if you got hurt before getting there. None of this was true, either. It was like one of those old armed forces commercials. He gave me this huge line that kind of seemed okay. It made me think maybe this is one of those deals that is true. But it wasn't.

"There were some good points about it but it doesn't look too good now. At the time it did, but now here I am at St. Ann's. None of that medical, pay or clothing did me any good and neither did the so-called training, because if it did, I wouldn't be here."

Jeff, 23, tells his story. "From May 1989 to October 1990, at first I wasn't sure about going to Job Corps. It had only been about a year since I was released from the Marine Corps on a medical discharge. I had a good job working construction, learning drywalling. Then one day I saw one of the Job Corps signs on the side of a bus. I went to ask about it and they told me they would send me to college. I thought it was great because I didn't think I was good enough for college; I wasn't good enough to be in high school. They built up my ego. I asked if there were any bad people there like gangs and they said, 'No, they're all like you. They really want to learn.' I asked if there were any jobs there and they said, 'Sure, you can have a job anytime you want. In fact, some people get jobs and live off center.' I said, 'Great.' I quit my job with the construction company and waited to go.

"It took about six months for me to get in Job Corps because they lost my paperwork twice. I had to move in with my parents and live there for about four months. Once at Job Corps it took me six more months to go into the college program. When

I first came I said I wanted to go in the college program and they said I couldn't do that. You have to stay and get a trade first. I said, 'I didn't come here for that. I came for college.' They said, 'Sorry, everybody has to get a trade.' I took a trade -- welding. I wanted electronics but they didn't have it at this center. I didn't finish welding. I waited for six months then dropped out and went into the college program.

"The Job Corps recruiters who got me to sign up didn't exactly lie to me, they just didn't tell me everything I needed to know. Later, I found out they gave me a little more information than some of the others who joined, especially people from LA. They just come and it's like a 180 degree turn from what they were told it was going to be.

"My first day in Job Corps was a little scary. When I got off that bus along with 93 others they said we were one of the largest groups of orientation students to come through. Then after they told us what was expected of us they took us to our dorm about 6:00 p.m. Then they put us in a room with other students, four to six to a room. The dorm was B Dorm. It had a large screen TV. It was nice; we had carpeting. I thought, *I can live with this.* You see, B Dorm is the orientation dorm, so after a week or so they packed us out and put us in other dorms. They put me in N Dorm. My Mexican friend went to G Dorm.

"Right off, the other students in the dorm started pestering me. But they didn't pester me too much because I was a big guy. They thought I would be too tough. The little guys got beat up and picked on all the time. To tell you the truth, some of those guys in the dorm I couldn't stand. They didn't come to Job Corps to learn, they just came to fight. I just didn't like them at all. They acted childish and foolish. Most of the time they were having pillow fights, getting drunk and puking all over the place. When you went to sleep they would put chili, hot peppers, Tabasco sauce, whatever in your mouth. They did it to me once. I didn't like it so I let them know about it. The next day I got tagged in the head by a big guy about seven feet tall who went by the name of 'Too Tall.' I hit him in the stomach a couple of times and knocked him over.

"There weren't a lot of authentic gangs, but there were a lot of guys claiming to be gang members. And along with their neighborhood homeboys they would try to put up a show. As for N Dorm, it was a pig sty. There was no carpeting on the floor. It was pretty dirty. The wallpaper looked old and there were few pictures on the walls. It didn't really please me. As for the residential advisors, I reserved my judgement on the RAs until I got to know them, but once I got to know them I wished I hadn't.

"After a little over a year on center I was terminated for not keeping my GPA up. I stayed in the area and after a year of working a part time job, I was able to get a grant to go to college. If I would have done that two years ago, I would have had two years of college in by now."

April was abused by her parents, not sexually at first, but mentally. They were Satan worshippers. April joined Job Corps when the juvenile court ordered her to stay in a group home until her 17th birthday for repeated shoplifting. Her family attorney was able to get her put on probation if she agreed to enlist in Job Corps. When she entered JC she continued to carry on the family tradition of Satan worship. She frequently invited students over her house on the weekends where, with the help of her parents, they were able to convert, using drugs and sexual acts with humans and animals. April was one of the lucky ones because eight months after joining Job Corps her parents were arrested on a drug related charge and were too preoccupied with their defense to continue entertaining April's friends on the weekends.

Two weeks later, during the Thanksgiving break, April and two of her male friends were picked up for shoplifting. Since her parents couldn't provide her and her friends with their weekly supply of drugs, to keep her small group of would-be Satan worshippers together she resorted to her old ways of getting something for nothing. But this time the authorities were able to uncover the abuse that April had been receiving over the years from her parents. With the help of the psychiatric care unit, they were able to provide the care that April needed.

She never completed a trade at Job Corps, but she did manage to get her GED. After getting out of reform school, she was able to get a job as a nurse's aid and took night classes. Now four years later April is an RN, mother of two, married to a Christian minister.

Turnabout Is Fair Play

I gotta tell you somth'n'. LA, New York, Washington, Vegas, Atlanta, etc. -- no matter where you are the Corps is out for more. The city's where I'm comin' from, other's all over the world. The city's a place where violence lurks everywhere, and the innocent are the most sinister. Madness everywhere, murder, robbery, rape, ain't nuttin' here. Drive-bys are at an all time dirty low. Politicians say crack is the reason things are as they are -- more cops, bigger guns and more laws are the cure. The last President said, "Just say no," while all the time he was lying, conniving and forgetting it all, helping the Contras with blood money made off the streets of the USA. Wouldn't you say? The new one is trying to sell us on a thousand points of light. If only we could see the light.

The man gave me just two ways out and I'm takin' number two. With ticket in hand I board the gray dog because the planes don't wanna fly, and I don't wanna die. The only thing I was guilty of was being born in the first place. Mamma said, "Pray to the Lord and He will help you. I love you, and don't forget to write." Right! So as I got off the dog, I said to myself, this place will be mine in a week or so because I'll be banging, ganging, dealing and doing all the wrong things trying to make this place just like home. The RAs give me negatives because that's what I was. Destruction was my middle name, aggravation was my game. Confined was how I felt. "You'd think this was a jail or som'n'," was what I said. But after that night, yes, I remember it so well -- that first night in the county jail. After that I appreciated the Corps all the more.

The dorm is quiet and the hallway deserted. How I long to hear my mother's voice, "Boy, do the right things before it's too late." That night I did a turn-around. The madness that possessed me had departed and I could see more clearly now. The rules are mine as written in black and white: do your Js, carry your ID, no smoking in the day room -- was my everyday thing. The different kinds of kids ranging on the race scale from top to bottom: white, black, hispanic, American Indian, Asian, Pacific islanders,

Vietnamese, Japanese and others I met. Talking to them helped make me see the world was not a battlefield, but just one big neighborhood. Bloods, Crips, Neo-Nazis, and the Forever More gangs don't last long here, but the child in a man's body could survive here. My time has passed.

I've done my J, and now it's time to move on to the real world with the help of behavioral modification, which in turn enabled me to have self control, determination, and motivation. It will make me live, live, live life to the fullest with all its ups and downs. I entered this place with the other 76 losers, but on my departure I was one of the six remaining. Now I am on my way back home after a stay of 18 months, ready to join the masses -- underpaid and overworked. But momentarily alive!

Illegal Activity

Gambling

Playing games of chance for money is another problem all together. Students will bet on just about anything -- craps (dice games), cards, sex, fights.

Drugs

Crack, smack, acid and pot are nothing when matched up against the power of alcohol. Controlling illegal substances in a Job Corps center has become a difficult thing to do. Stopping them from entering the centers is impossible. To pass Job Corps' mandatory drug testing, students using drugs stop taking drugs prior to entering just long enough to allow the drugs to work themselves out of the system. Alcohol abuse has been the number one problem on Job Corps center, and it looks like it will always be number one.

A new student will have no problem finding or buying drugs on or off most centers because the same rules of drug dealing that apply on the street change very little on centers. Everything can be bought for the right price. Drugs, sex (male or female), stolen goods, things that can be traded. Drugs are also used to make others behave in ways they would not otherwise behave. For instance, if a student would like someone to beat up or kill you, name it. For the right price or drugs it's no problem. A large number of white students from the upper Rockies -- Montana, North and South Dakota, Idaho and Utah -- are heavy metal listeners and use inhalants like glue, lighter fluid, paint thinner and all types of aerosol sprays. The users of inhalants are referred to as glue heads, sniffers or poppers. Also available are hallucinogenics like LSD and PCP, as well as marijuana or grass, pot, reefer. Name your poison -- they're all here.

A little of the drug language most commonly used by the students today:

Hit, pull, drag -- drug dose
Acid -- LSD
Acid head -- LSD user
Buss, high, boss high, stoned, trip or tripping -- drug-induced intoxication
Bag, baggies -- plastic bag of drugs
Angel dust -- PCP
Crack -- smokable form of cocaine
Crank -- amphetamines
Crashing -- drug withdrawal
Croke -- a mixture of speed, cocaine and methamphetamine
Drop -- a drop of acid on a piece of paper
Duster -- cigarette made of marijuana, tobacco or parsley, sprinkled with PCP
Downers -- tranquilizers
Grass, hash, ganja, dope, pot, weed -- all forms or marijuana, most of the time
Ice, crystal -- methamphetamine
Roach -- tail end of a marijuana cigarette
Rush -- feeling of exhilaration produced by drug intoxication
Speed freak -- someone who takes uppers and downers
Rock house -- a place to get drugs
Red birds, reds, goff balls -- barbiturates
Uppers -- amphetamines

The drug language changes with every tick of the clock and sometimes it seems like a full-time job just trying to keep informed.

Student Rights

The centers are security paid employees of the contractors. At times, you may feel you have entered a world without human rights. But you, the student, have more ways of getting help than you can imagine. Write a letter, make call. Don't just sit there! Free yourself from the pain of injustices. Many students are afraid to speak out against Job Corps in fear of being terminated from the program. If you are arrested on or off center, know your rights -- the Miranda Rights.

First, you have the right not to answer any question, except to supply your name, age, address and the name of your parent or guardian. If the police use force or intimidation to force you to talk, it's illegal. Second, you have the right to call your parents or lawyer or both. If you do not have a lawyer, you have the right to ask for one. Third, you have the right to stop answering questions at any time, or to wait until your lawyer arrives before continuing. Job Corps security makes arrests, takes a student into custody and holds him in a detention cell known as room two without reading his rights or informing his parents.

Your First Week of Job Corps

Orientation Schedule

Tuesday -- day 1. Four or more days a month or one or more days a week are referred to as orientation days. Orientation days are the days new students arrive between the hours of 6:00 a.m. and 1 a.m. that night, depending on what time their plane or bus gets in.

1. On arrival, students will attend an orientation session with orientation staff. This is their welcoming and information session used for completion of forms, inventory of personal property and issuing of lock and toiletry kit. Then they are transported to the dormitories if after 3 or 4 p.m.
2. Welcome to the dormitory. Meeting with the RAs. At that time, student will complete more forms, receive room and locker assignment, information on protection of personal property, fire safety, general dorm rules, then unpack and settle in.
3. Meeting with counselor, safe arrival call to home, setting up appointments for intake interview and initial group session. If time allows you may tour campus and visit recreation area.
4. 10:00 p.m. weekdays -- dorm group meeting with all the students living in the dormitory, introduction of new dorm members. After group, some dorm clean-up, then bed time. At 11:00 p.m. lights out, end of the day.

Wednesday -- day 2.

6:00 a.m. Wake up. All students up by 6:30 a.m. Dorm morning clean up, breakfast.

8:00 a.m. Report to orientation room for the following information: explanation of medical services available, medical examination, roll call, question and answer period, student handbook review, rules of conduct, tour of the campus, initial living allowance (around $10 to new enrollees). If you have not made your safe arrival call home, contact your counselor.

5:00 p.m. Dinner time.

9:00 p.m. Meeting with dorm advisor, discussion of dorm rules, pass system, laundry, grooming, etc.

10:00 p.m. Dorm group -- all students must attend. Introduction of late arrivals, dorm information, dorm clean up, then bed time.

11:00 p.m. Lights out, end of day.

Thursday -- day 3.

6:00 a.m. Wake up. Clean up dorm room and make bed, breakfast.

8:00 a.m. Back to orientation, roll call, briefing on the schedule for the day. Discussion of disciplinary system, review boards, appeal rights and procedures. Safety presentation including methods to correct and/or avoid safety hazards.

11:30 a.m. Lunch

12:30 p.m. Human sexuality presentation, discussion of recreation activities available, students complete recreation activities participation plan.

3:30 p.m. Dormitories open.

5:00 p.m. Dinner time. Cafeteria open until 6:30 p.m.

9:00 p.m. Meeting with dorm advisor, training on use and maintenance of dorm equipment washers, dryers, irons, buffers, etc.

10:00 p.m. Dorm group -- all students must attend. Introduction of late arrivals, dorm information, dorm clean up then bed time.

11:00 p.m. Lights out, end of day.

Friday -- day 4.

6:00 a.m. Wake up. Clean up dorm and room, make bed, breakfast.

8:00 a.m. Back to orientation, roll call, briefing on the schedule for the day. Discussion on cultural awareness and state laws, sexual harassment.
11:30 a.m. Lunch
12:30 p.m. Roll call, water safety.
3:30 p.m. Dormitories open, leisure time.
5:00 p.m. Dinner time. Cafeteria open until 6:30 p.m.
12:00 a.m. Bed check, lights out, center movie playing, end of day.
1:00 a.m. to 2:00 a.m. Dorm down for the night.

Saturday -- day 5.
8:00 a.m. Wake up for orientation students only. Make bed, clean room, breakfast.
9:00 a.m. to 4:30 p.m. Tour of the city, visit museum, lunch at local restaurant.
5:00 p.m. Dinner back on center.
12:00 a.m. Bed check, lights out, center movie playing, end of day.
1:00 a.m. to 2:00 a.m. Dorm down for the night.

Sunday -- day 6.
8:00 a.m. Breakfast for students going to church. There are no churches on center, but the center has a bus that will drop you off in town so you can attend the church of your choice in the local community.
11:00 a.m. All students wake up, room and dorm clean up. Brunch, leisure time.
5:00 p.m. Dinner.
10:00 p.m. Dorm clean up, bed time.
11:00 p.m. Lights out, end of day.

Monday -- day 7.
5:00 a.m. Orientation students have to wake up earlier than the rest of the other students in the dorm because they are required to work in the cafeteria for one week.

6:00 a.m. Dorm wake up. Breakfast, all students up by 6:30 a.m., dorm morning clean up, breakfast.
8:00 a.m. Report to orientation, roll call, testing in math and reading.
11:30 a.m. Lunch.
12:30 p.m. Orientation roll call, question and answer period. Cultural awareness meeting.
3:30 p.m. Dormitories open.
4:00 p.m. Dorm group meeting -- all students must attend.
5:00 p.m. Dinner time. Cafeteria open until 6:30 p.m.
9:00 p.m. Meeting with dorm advisor, training on dorm cleanliness and dorm scores, personal hygiene and appearance.
10:00 p.m. Dorm group -- all students must attend. Dorm information, dorm clean up, then bed time.
11:00 p.m. Lights out, end of day.

The ages on center have started at 15 and end at 26 even though the Job Corps enrollment rules state Job Corps enrolls kids between 16 and 22. The Job Corps recruiter and the kids themselves have found a way to get around this by signing people up right until their 22nd birthday. By using this tactic, an entering student could be a lot older than the majority of the students.

Checklist for a Better Center

If you have to go to Job Corps this checklist will help you get into one of the better ones.

1. Find out from the start what Job Corps center you will be attending. Don't let the screener win you over with a lot of pretty pictures of a place you may or may not have heard of. Ask for references of prior students. Phone them and ask them questions. How did they like the center? Was the screener up front, truthful and direct about the center you are about to attend? How were the food, living and sanitary conditions? Are the living conditions just like they are in the pictures the screener showed?
2. Check your local library for books on Job Corps and its programs. Read everything you can find.
3. Never attend a center with more than 500 students because you may find the centers with the most students are more into quantity than quality in their programs.
4. Never attend a center under the control of a contractor that is under investigation. The government agency responsible for all Job Corps centers is the Department of Labor (DOL). They operate some of the centers themselves but the majority of the larger centers are contracted out to management corporations like Management and Training Corporation (MTC) of Ogden, Utah.
5. It's always a good idea to record or get in writing the guarantees the Job Corps recruiter has given you on the job training you have chosen before signing the entry papers.
6. There are as many as 100 Job Corps centers throughout the United States. Try to stay at home in your own state or part of the country because going to a center out of your area makes for a long and dangerous walk home

for whatever negative reasons you decide to leave the program.

7. Be suspicious of anyone and everyone.
8. Ask the recruiter for a copy of the Job Corps center rules and regulations for the center you will be attending.

I have found there're a number of parents who are very concerned about their children once they have enrolled into the Job Corps program. They find themselves wondering what they should do next to help make sure their son or daughter is doing okay. Also there're some parents who wait until it's too late before they contact their children or the center they are attending to find out how they are doing. Here are some tips I truly believe will help you and your son or daughter through the adjustment process. I have also found most students do a lot better in their school and trade when their parents heed the following suggestions:

1. Know where to reach your child day or night.
2. Call your son or daughter once a week. Have him/her give you the number to the dormitory, then arrange to call at a set time each week making sure to never take longer than five minutes.
3. Give your child a number where you can be reached day or night.
4. Make it clear to your child that he/she is only to call in case of emergencies.
5. Familiarize yourself with Job Corps rules and regulations. Check with your Job Corps recruiter. He should be more than happy to help.
6. Reward your child with a gift not money.
7. Be alert to the signs of drug or alcohol abuse.
8. Take an active interest in your child's extra curricular activities, academics, love life, etc.

9. Make a point to call and talk to the counselors,
residential advisors, teachers. Ask them questions about
your child's behavior and progress.
10. Encourage your child to be independent.

Religious Worship

The moral outlook of Job Corps is one that should concern us all. Morality shouldn't be looked upon as something we can turn on when we feel the need to do right or turn off when we want to party. Weekends and pay days are the hardest times of all for Job Corps students. A student with money, no matter how much, will most often find himself the target of drug, alcohol and sex peddlers. It doesn't matter how young, or if one is male or female, if he has cash, his friends will show him the way.

Job is the main character in the Book of Job of the Old Testament. It ranks among the finest examples of Hebrew poetry. It tell of Satan's attempt to destroy Job's faith in God. Satan insists that Job is a righteous man only because God rewards him for it with prosperity. God then gives Job into the power of Satan, who destroys his riches, afflicts him with disease, kills his family and tries him to the utmost. But Job never loses his patience, and the phrase "the patience of Job" is commonly used to this day.

Hate, Bitterness, Hurt

Worship is never as important to MTC as their primary objective -- money. There is never a peaceful moment a person can have alone to consult with one's God. I have noticed when a student is following his religious faith, reading his Bible and religious material, he is more inclined to complete the task at hand and is less likely to harm others or commit crimes while on Job Corps centers. A student going through the Job Corps training program has a lot of things going on inside his mind -- things that he may or may not have had to deal with before in his life.

And from this increased brain activity comes problems and difficulties only one's religious faith may be able to help one through. You, as a parent, can be of great help to your child now more than you could ever imagine. Inform your spiritual leader that your child is in Job Corps. Give him a phone number so he may contact your child. Send spiritual materials -- Bible, books, pamphlets, etc. "Don't let the evil win."

I have found some of the kids entering Job Corps have connections with devil worshippers. These cults are few, but church attendance is low as well. The demonic influence can be felt in the late hours of the night, as our babies cry themselves to sleep.

Get the name and address of your screener so you can keep him informed of your progress, likes and dislikes about the center you are attending. If you are under the age of 18 you may wish to contact your state children's services agencies or the local children's services. Your congressional representatives back home usually have an 800 number that may save you the cost of the call. If you do not have this information handy, call a relative or friend back home and ask him to look up the names, addresses, and telephone numbers in your local telephone directory under city, state and government agencies. Call or write the director of the U.S. Department of Labor, 196 Stout Street, Denver, CO 80294, (303)844-4807 or (303)844-5061, your local Department of Labor Office or the main office of the Department of Labor in Washington, D.C. Write me, the author of this book at 422 West 4800 South, Washington Terrace, Utah 84405. I would be more than happy to help you.

Job Corps was started in hopes that its programs would help the poor and lower class people of the United States out of the never ending poverty merry-go-round they are on, but after over two decades, the problems of unemployment and poor living conditions have shown little or no improvement. In fact, through the help of the Job Corps program, we have increased gang membership, as well as drugs and crime. Job Corps is not a deterrent for crime or a rehabilitation center for drug users. The kids aren't sentenced there, but sign on the dotted line. Some of the young men and very few of the women do complete the program and return to their home towns to become productive taxpaying citizens. The success of the young men and women isn't due so much to the Job Corps' program but to the drive and determination of the individual.

The End